More letters to **GROWING PAINS**

Phillip Hodson is Britain's best-known agony uncle. He appears regularly on BBC1 and TVS programmes and has his own phone-in problem programme on LBC Newstalk radio each afternoon in London. He is the agony uncle of *Family Circle* magazine and writes the popular *Talk About It!* column every week in *Fast Forward*. Phillip is a fully qualified counsellor and his previous books include *Men – An investigation into the emotional male* (BBC Books, 1984) and *Letters to Growing Pains* (BBC Books, 1988). He lives in London with his son (11), fellow-counsellor Anne Hooper, friends, a cat called Orbit and a lot of old electric trains.

For my Dad (1917–1990)

Published by BBC Books,
a division of BBC Enterprises Limited,
Woodlands, 80 Wood Lane, London W12 0TT
First published 1990

ISBN 0 563 36122 0

Set in 11/12 pt Baskerville by
Ace Filmsetting Ltd, Frome, Somerset
Printed and bound in Great Britain by Clays Ltd, St Ives Plc
Cover printed by Clays Ltd, St Ives Plc

MORE
LETTERS TO
GROWING
PAINS

Phillip Hodson

BBC BOOKS

ACKNOWLEDGEMENTS

To Cathy Gilbey, Chris Bellinger, Nicky Smith and all at the Beeb, especially Sarah Greene for being so kind.

To my son Alexander for his wisdom in choosing the letters and the rest of the family for understanding my deadlines. To Anne and Linda for their continual support. Special thanks to all who wrote to Growing Pains and Talk About It! This is your book.

CONTENTS

	Introduction	6
1	Love me do	9
2	Periods, breasts and bras	39
3	Other bodily problems	53
4	My bad habits	71
5	About death and sadness	83
6	Stop teasing me!	95
7	Trouble with my family and friends	107
8	Doing schoolwork	133
9	Fears and attacks	141
10	Extras	151

Introduction

This is a new book of some of the letters (about 3 per cent!) sent to BBC 1's *Going Live!* programme and my column in *Fast Forward* magazine, together with my replies. I've produced it because on TV or in print there's never enough time or space to cover all the subjects in one go. As soon as we've talked about family rows, it's time to discuss teasing again. So, whatever your problem, this book gives you the answers in a single collection.

I've also written it because nobody seems to understand that children are changing. When I was a lad (as they say), I got interested in girls and clothes at 16. When my stepsons were lads, they got interested at 14. These days, thanks to the impact of films and television, it happens from 9 years on, as your letters and my 11-year-old son tell me. Hence my big chapter at the start called LOVE ME DO, about managing a romance.

Equally important is the subject of PERIODS, BREASTS AND BRAS. Mums and Dads and schools are still not telling girls enough about the changes happening inside their bodies when periods begin. If you don't believe me, read the letters in this book. I understand that adults get embarrassed when their girls become women, but it really isn't good enough to avoid the subject. It's cruel not to answer young people's questions.

I'm also inundated with letters about teasing and I think you'll find lots of varied answers in the section called STOP TEASING ME! However, this is one problem you can't really expect the grown-ups to solve. It isn't good for you to be protected from every irritation in life. On the other hand, the chapters ABOUT DEATH AND SADNESS and TROUBLE

WITH MY FAMILY AND FRIENDS do encourage you to get emotional support at times when life isn't irritating but plain overwhelming.

Finally, the letters from children who have been attacked or abused are a reminder *always* to demand help when risky adults pose a threat. I'm glad to say that in every case where we've talked about these matters on TV, the children concerned have been helped to safety (see the chapter on FEARS AND ATTACKS), and that makes me proud.

CHAPTER 1

Love me do

Love tingle

I really like a boy who I see quite often. When I think about him I get a tingle all over and my legs, feet and arms seem cold without actually being cold. It's like what I get before Christmas Day or when you're nervous. My friend fancies him too but it's a secret between us. Do I really love him? I am only ten and so is he. Please help. A Confused Girl.

People use the word love to mean different things.

In the best sense, you love someone because you've had a good chance to get to know them. At present, it's probably more accurate to say you *fancy* this boy. He gives you a definite physical thrill of pleasure and excitement. It might turn into love one day, but only when you discover whether he pleases your mind as well as your body. What if he tortures frogs? Or picks his nose? Or hates girls?

Some of these things might just matter to you.

Fatal attraction?

I have the biggest problem in the world. I knew this boy in my class. He fancied me something mad. He asked me out. I blushed and said Yes. I went to his house. We were watching Fatal Attraction *when he tried to kiss me. Next day when I went to school I noticed he wasn't in his usual seat. Have I scared him off? Please advise. Anon, aged 13.*

Most likely, he has flu or some other good reason for not being at school. I doubt he feels too embarrassed. (That's really what *you* are feeling, isn't it?)

Of course, it's just possible he's in trouble for

showing you his parents' videos, but I don't think the punishment would be a holiday!

Try to accept that sometimes you get a bit out of your depth. It's OK to feel scared, even at 13; just take things more slowly.

Asking him out

I am 11 and have just started secondary school with all my friends. There are loads from our old class and there's this boy that I really fancy. Everyone gets on with him. I have tried to be partners with him in some subjects so I can ask him out but I'm embarrassed about it. I don't know what to say or how to go about it. Everyone gets on with him because he's funny and always cheers you up if you're glum. Please tell me what to do, I'm desperate. FF fan.

This is the number one problem in my *FF* postbag so don't think you're alone. And naturally you feel embarrassed when trying to approach a boy for the first time.

You get hot and bothered because you feel anxious. 'I'm too excited to think straight. My heart's pounding. I'm afraid he will reject me and that others will laugh.'

OK – work out what you want to say – 'Can we walk home together today? I really like being with you.' Tell him this when he has enough time to answer and no one will overhear. Be ready for him to say no or yes, so you can prepare your own reactions. If it's a 'no', say: 'Is that a permanent no, or just a "no" for now?' When you've made this approach, say how nervous you felt about doing it. It will help calm you. Remember to keep breathing slowly and regularly throughout so you don't dry up. And have a nice time.

Asking her out

My problem is girls – they won't go out with me. I try to talk to them and do everything that pleases them but they just ignore me. I wear aftershave and stuff like that. It is embarrassing because all the other boys in my class are going out with girls. What can I do? Anon.

This is the second biggest problem in my *FF* postbag! The tough answer is that girls don't go out with bottles of aftershave. They go out with people. Smelling nice helps, but that won't do the trick by itself.

You need to concentrate on natural behaviour rather than a plot. In order to get a girlfriend, you have to be *genuinely* interested in her. That means talking about her life, feelings, hopes, wishes and fears. This means listening well, reacting and smiling. You actually have to concentrate! It's an advantage if you can be funny but don't worry if you can't. Practise having better conversations with your family and friends to begin with.

How to kiss   1

I am 15 years old and I have never French-kissed before and I am scared that when I have to French-kiss anyone I will not know what to do. Anonymous Girl.

People have written books on the art of kissing but the elements are simple.

Be sensitive. Vary your pace. Sometimes it's exciting to think the other person cannot wait to get at you. More often it's fun to be teased a bit. Lips should be touched lightly as well as firmly. Dry skin is rough. Dribbling is a turn-off. Nibbling is nice. Banging teeth together can lead to expensive dentistry. Blowing into your partner's lungs can be a shock. Using your mouth like a Hoover likewise.

The tongue also comes into play – usually – to French-kiss. Normally, you work up to this, rather than jump in straight away, and you tend to make sure you know the person quite well.

Like everything, it's your choice whether you do it. There's no compulsion. And you won't want to do it twice with someone who does not clean his teeth properly or who has bad breath.

All that happens is that as you kiss, your lips gradually part and your tongue sneaks slowly forward. If the other person opens up, then you tend to push further, and in their turn, so do they. But there's no correct method – it's just exploration.

Practise, if you like, by French-kissing your own clenched fist. You'll soon get the hang of it.

How to kiss   2

I have got a crush on a girl in my school. She keeps asking me to kiss her. I say no because I am not sure how to do any kind of kiss. I am also afraid if I do not kiss her soon I might lose her. Please tell me how to do every kind of kiss. Paul, aged 11.

I don't have enough space to tell you how to do *every* kind of kiss, and we did write about French-kissing a few weeks ago, but here goes for the kiss 'basic'.

Put your lips lightly together, making sure they are neither too wet nor too dry (lick them, then rub them with your hand). Bend your head to your right while your partner bends her head to your left (otherwise noses will collide) and gently lean forward till your closed lips meet hers. Squeeze the muscles at the sides of your lips so that your mouth puckers into a small mound while your partner does the same. Move your head around a little so the point of contact is varied. As the kiss comes to an end, very softly suck inwards over your lips and separate them to make a delicate kissing sound.

How to kiss 3

My problem is that I don't know how to kiss (snog) and I don't go out with boys because of it. I know in your replies you have told other people what to do but my question is where do you put your tongue? I need to know and I can't ask my parents. Big FF fan, aged 13.

Before talking about tongues, let's just say you don't *have* to snog in order to go out with boys. You can choose!

But if you are going to start kissing soon, it's perfectly reasonable to wonder where the tongues fit in.

The first few times, I suggest you keep your tongue in your mouth and kiss with the faintest pressure of lips only, slowly and gently.

As you get to know each other better, you might open your mouth just a little and let your tongue flick your boyfriend's lips. Later, people get more involved and French-kiss, almost 'swapping' tongues inside each other's mouths.

However, the important thing about kissing is not to become world champion, but to be sensitive to skin sensation. Touch your own arm with your fingernail slowly and see what I mean.

Hates kissing

I think there is something wrong with me. I am 12 but cannot kiss or show my affections to anyone. To me, it is disgusting and sickening. I can't understand how anyone can enjoy it. I have been out with boys and given them a peck on the cheek but I can't bring myself to kiss them. I don't think I have ever fallen in love with anyone, and that's my secret. Is it because I have never been loved by a boy so can't imagine what it is like? I don't even want to know how love feels. John Leslie fan.

I'd be worried if you said no one in your family loved you. Or if you said you could never show any affection to your parents or friends or even the family dog.

But I don't think there's anything wrong with you just because you can't kiss boys at 12. You are just saying you aren't ready yet, and nor is your body. (I couldn't believe the facts of life when I first heard them either – yuk!) We all develop feelings at different rates and I promise you'll realise when you are ready to love a boyfriend.

When to kiss

I've got a big problem. I love girls but when I tell my Mum and Dad they make jokes about me and say not to get too serious (I am 10). I am going out with a girl at the moment and I don't know when to kiss her. NKOTB fan.

Yes, I love girls too. I expect your Dad feels the same way. If not, how did he ever meet your Mum?

Your parents are finding it hard to adjust to you growing up. I suggest you humour them. Let them tease you just a little. After all, you don't want to settle down too early, do you?

As for kissing, why not talk to your girlfriend? She's got a say in this as well.

Madly in love

I fancy one of the boys in my class but he just doesn't want to know me. I've tried so many times to get his attention but it's always the same answer. No! I've got to the stage of asking my parents to move me to a different school. I've told some people but they just laughed saying I was silly and will get over it. What shall I do? I love him so much! Madly In Love Teenager.

You're not silly. Love is real. But you have to accept his no as a no. Tell yourself to give him up as a bad job. When you do, perhaps you would like to cry, or shout, or sulk? That's the way to get over someone – letting your hair down.

Made to kiss

I have just started going out with boys. The other kids already spend all their time kissing. My two friends and I don't want to, but the others hold our arms and push us towards our boyfriends. We are only 11 and don't want to get too involved yet. Plus if we don't kiss they call us chickens and tight. What shall we do? NKOTB fan.

Tell them you'd rather be a chicken than join a flock of sheep because *you* will decide when to kiss someone, and in private.

Finding a fella

My problem is I'm trying to find a boyfriend. I have not had much luck since I was six.

Please can you give me some good advice about what I should do? Jessie, Cirencester (12).

Your letter makes me think you had a good time in primary school! But I'm sure you mean you feel you've been cut off from boys for years.

You cannot go out and buy a boyfriend. You can only increase your chances of someone coming your way.

First, mix more. It's a basic point even grown-ups overlook. But unless you're meeting lots of people you are unlikely to make really close friends. Quantity matters.

Second, be more effective when you mix. Learn to look people in the eye, smile and take an interest in them. Ask them general questions which don't easily end in a 'yes' or 'no'. For instance, it's better to say 'How are things?' than 'Have you got an orang-utan in your satchel?' Taking an interest in people's views really counts.

Third and last, be patient. You can't win 'em all. Some people won't like you and you wouldn't be really human if everyone did (you'd be a sort of saint).

Lies to parents

I have been going out with my boyfriend for seven weeks now but my parents don't know. I am 15 and my boyfriend is 20. I am afraid to tell my parents because I know that they won't approve because of the age-gap. I am really fond of Pete, my boyfriend, and I'm not going to let my parents split us up. Seeing each other is a problem. Tuesdays and Thursdays he picks me up from school and we usually go back to his house until his Mum and Dad get in from work. We usually see each other once at the weekend. I tell my parents that I am going out with a girlfriend. I think my parents might be suspicious. Should I tell them about Pete or not? His parents don't know either. Miss X, West of England.

Living a set of lies is always difficult and when you get found out you appear to have been immature. The age-gap is quite big now which is why your parents may feel anxious, although it will seem less to everyone in a couple of years' time. If you're ready to prove that this relationship matters, then why not start by confiding in Pete's family? Tell them your worries and wishes. If they could approach your parents *with you*, there's a better chance that everyone will take you seriously and you'll get what you want.

Does he love me?

Please help me. I really LOVE this boy, but every time I go to talk or something he walks away and says he'll talk to me later but he never does. Do you think that he loves me at all? If not, what should I do to get him to love me? A desperate Jason Donovan fan.

I think he's rude, or shy, or both. But I can't know whether he loves you or not. Only he can say. You need to know where you stand and take control. So next time he tries to walk off, say: 'Wait a minute. Would you really like to be friends and talk, or am I bothering you? Tell me so I can know what to do?' He will like you if he feels comfortable with you and putting him more at ease should help.

Rat

I am 13 years old and have a bit of a problem. There's a boy at school that I'm really attracted to and he knows I am, but he takes advantage of this for getting money and other things from me. I don't know what to do because I fancy him so much and haven't got the heart to tell him to go away. Lonely Girl.

Well, *he's* got no heart or he wouldn't be cashing in on your loneliness. In a sad sort of way, you've been reduced to buying his attention. This tells me just how lonely you feel. It also tells me you don't know how to solve your problem. Please stop thinking you are worthless. If you feel inferior, that is because someone has been getting at you. (Maybe this bloke?) Or you blame all your loneliness on yourself. Anyone can get lonely by staying at home and becoming afraid to make new friends. Make the decision to circulate more. Look people in the eye. Smile more. Breathe in before you speak. Plan what you want to say. This will give you lots more confidence. Enough confidence to tell this guy he's cheap at any price.

Wants her friend's fella

I am 13 and in love with my best friend's boyfriend. She has just had an argument with him and I am considering asking him out. Last week, he walked me and my friend home and then when we got to my house he then kissed me. I want to know whether to ask him out or to leave it. Please help me. Anna – worried and in love.

If you ask him out without telling your best friend, she will probably never speak to you again. (Think of how you'd feel if the situations were reversed!)

If you ask him out *after* telling your best friend, she still may never speak to you again.

You have to decide how important her friendship really is, because there's certainly a chance that she might chuck you.

So you decide if the risk is worth it. Find out how badly they are getting on because it's just possible she might be pleased to see the back of him.

Octopus

I am 12 years old and have a 14-year-old boyfriend. Because he is much older, he thinks I have been through the same things as him. When I am at his house, he tries to feel me in unspeakable places. He is really nice but I don't know how I can keep going out with him. I can't tell my Mum, because I don't know what she would say. Please help me! From a NKOTB fan.

I'm sorry you can't tell your Mum because it would be nice to have her on your side.

What she would probably say is that loving someone does *not* mean always doing what they want.

You've made it perfectly clear, in a sensible way, that you aren't comfortable with your boyfriend's behaviour.

Loving you should mean that he won't force you. So ask him to be nicer still and keep his hands to himself.

Going further

I am 15 years old and I am going out with a 17-year-old boy. He is really nice and we get on well. We have kissed and stuff but we haven't actually got off yet. He

says he will use the necessary precautions (condoms).
But I am not sure if I want to go ahead with it. Please
help. In Love.

If you are not sure you want to go ahead, then you
are *NOT* ready, apart from the fact that *he* will be
breaking the law if you do. It's really best to wait
until you want this more than anything in the
world!

Silent love

I am in love with a girl who is older than me and I
hardly know her. I think she likes me. I am 11. Please
give me some advice. Stuart, Plymouth.

Then get to know her. It's jolly difficult walking up
to a stranger and saying, 'I love you.' By compari-
son, it would be easy to nod, smile, offer her a bit
of your chocolate and ask her what she thought
about last night's telly (or Bros, or *Fast Forward*, or
horoscopes, etc.). She may not respond, but you
won't get anywhere by worshipping from afar, will
you?

Then if you click, you can become more personal (but not during the first chat – give it a while).

Love, or crush?

A few weeks ago, I went on holiday to Spain and there I
fell in love with the waiter that sometimes served us. My
Dad told him that I liked him and a few times he kissed
me for fun. This made leaving him feel so much worse. I
have been home for four weeks now and I can't stop
thinking about him. I keep looking at his photo and
wishing I was still there with him. A few times I have
had dreams about him and every time someone mentions

his name I keep wanting to cry as I know I cannot see him again till next year. My Mum says it is just a crush and I will get over it. But I know I am really in love with him and I don't know what to do. I know he isn't married but he is a few years older than me and I know it can't work out, but this doesn't change the way I feel. Help! LT.

Your feelings are real. Love is love is love. It can hurt at any age. So don't ignore what has happened (as if you could!). You say yourself there are practical obstacles. But that doesn't mean you can't think, pine, talk, smile, wish, hope, write, sing, shout and cry. What your Mum should really do (tell her) is encourage you to enjoy this feeling of love even if it can't take you to Spain just yet. I promise it won't kill you not having him. But it will upset you to be told you're being silly, so fight back.

Crushes

I am 12 years old and I have this crush on this boy. He's really good-looking and most of the girls like him. I go to an all-girls' school and he goes to a boys'. We have a lesson on Mondays and Fridays where we are mixed. I am not in his class. But when I go to the boys' school, I sometimes pass him when he goes to the girls' school. And I can't concentrate on my work because I keep on thinking about him. I don't know if he's got a crush on me. From an Unknown.

It's usually quite nice to have crushes. Even if it isn't, you start feeling like this at around 12. So tell yourself two things. What's happened is natural yet it also seems strange because it's new. Give yourself time to get used to the idea.

So far you only know this boy from a distance. He may actually *not* be fun. But the only way to find out is if you start talking to him. And the only way to get your mind back on your work, is when you've dealt with these feelings first.

Close girls

I have a problem. I am a girl; and I fancy a girl at school and once I kissed her. She told all her friends. Now I am so embarrassed. It has got to the point where I bunk off school. What shall I do? A desperate Kylie fan.

Well, stop bunking off school because that means you really are ashamed of yourself.

You can't help feeling this way and it's not so unusual to get attached to close friends, so don't give yourself grief.

The real embarrassment is the mob. They can't deal with their own reaction.

So why do you help them? Just walk past. Just be yourself.

What's 'going out'?

Please, please help me. Recently, a boy asked me out and I did not know whether to say yes or no. I said yes, but the problem is I don't know what 'going out' means. Does it mean I will go out with him to a place or does it mean we just love each other from now on? Please help. I am 10. I do not see how anybody at my age could go to places with anybody when they are so young. Puzzled at 10.

And you're right. *Going out with/going with* usually means you've become best friends with someone of the opposite sex. So no one is expecting you to announce you're off to New York for a weekend alone with your fella. However, don't let anyone push you around. If you keep saying yes before you know what the question means, you could end up in all sorts of pickles, couldn't you?

Distant lovers

I have been friendly with this girl for about a year and a half and I am very keen on her and would like to go out with her. The trouble is I live in Bristol and she lives in Manchester. Is it possible to go out with somebody when they live so far away and if so what will it involve? DG.

It's possible. You must have overcome some of the distance to be friendly at all. But it's not convenient. First, you wouldn't be able to meet often – the journey takes hours. Second, travel is expensive – I don't know if you're rich, but you'd need to be. Third, it's difficult to stay in *enough* touch. You sort of lose closeness. Try it if you both want, writing and phoning, but the signs aren't good.

Love of lies

I'm 15½ years old and have never had a boyfriend. I've never admitted this to anyone else but in June last year I decided to say that I had met this lad that I really liked and was going out with him. I had planned on telling everyone that I'd fallen out with him after a few weeks or so but my telling lies got out of hand and I carried on making up stories about our relationship. This carried on for about a year, in the course of which this boy 'died' (to get me out of introducing him to people) but by then I'd invented other friends and relatives of his. I've lied so much and I know one of my real friends knows it isn't true. I feel extremely guilty and I cannot face telling everyone that I've lied to them. Please help. Anon.

You don't have to confess, you know, that's just your guilty feeling. If anyone asks about all these invented people, just say it's a closed chapter, it's painful, you don't want to talk about it. Try to forgive yourself not for telling the lies but for the need on which the lies were based. You've learned the hard way that lying gets very complicated – to be successful, you have to be a genius and remember all your tall stories. But you were feeling shy, left out and lonely – and that's nothing to be ashamed of. Start afresh.

Gets fresh

I have a problem. I fancy a boy called M . . . . . and he has just asked me out. I said yes. But last week he invited me to his house. When I got there, he pushed me onto his bed and started getting fresh. I pushed him off and walked out. I see him every day at school and every time I look at him and he says 'Just you wait', I don't know what to do. Please help. Fiona, Glasgow.

You clearly like M, but not his behaviour which is rude and crude. You need to educate him as well as yourself.

Instead of putting up with these threatening, smouldering looks, go and talk to him. Say you did not like being jumped on the other day and it upset you. Tell him what a bad move it was if he wants a girlfriend.

Then see if he'd like to come round to your house (when you know someone else will be on the premises). If he's really worth pursuing, he'll be able to cope. If not, forget it.

Now pregnant 1

I am a 16-year-old and I have had my period for five years. Two months ago, I went with my boyfriend and had a bit too much to drink at the party. We went back to his place. I have just found out that I am pregnant. I haven't told anyone. What shall I do? Have an abortion, or tell my Mum? My boyfriend dumped me three weeks ago. Very Depressed.

Whatever happens you need adult help, so please try to talk to your Mum. Don't expect her to be thrilled, but ask her if she will see you through. (If it's very difficult, tell your doctor you need basic support in breaking the news to your parents.) Remember, you're not on your own even if your boyfriend has walked out.

Now pregnant 2

Please help me, I don't know what to do. I think I'm pregnant only I can't make sure because my Mum is certain to find out because she just knows everybody. She even found out when my sister went on the pill when she went to see her doctor. What can I do? I'm only 15 and my boyfriend is 16. I think it's supposed to be illegal to have sex with a girl under 16 so I can't tell my Mum or she will chuck me out of the house. My boyfriend and I love each other so much and he understands me but he doesn't know what to do. Help. Belinda Carlisle fan.

First, let me assure you that the law takes no interest in prosecuting 16-year-old boys for sleeping with their girlfriends. So please reconsider telling your Mum what has happened.

Second, you need to find out whether you are pregnant or not. If you fear your GP is not the person to talk to, get properly checked out at any Family Planning Clinic or the Brook Advisory Service (look in the phone book for the nearest numbers). There are also home pregnancy testing kits available from the chemist.

Third, if you *are* pregnant you will need adult help whatever happens. If you just wish the problem away, you will find you've become a mother by next summer. Then everyone will know, so the question is not *whether* you tell but *when* and *how*.

I think it's often best to ask another grown-up to help you speak to your parents so any rage from them can be contained. This might be your doctor or someone from the clinic.

But – please act quickly. The more you delay, the more your health is at risk however the future is decided.

Does he like me?

I have a crush on a boy and I think he likes me. But I am not sure, *so I don't know whether to ask him out. I would like you to try and help me decide if he likes me. I will not ask him out unless I am* certain *he likes me. Puzzled Teenager.*

The whole trouble is you can *never* be sure that a stranger really likes you. Even if they do, they might play a game and not admit it, or pretend they do when they don't.

So if you wait till you are *absolutely certain* before speaking, you will *never* get your mouth open, and never go out.

I know you are afraid of rejection. But embarrassment won't kill you, so take a chance.

If he says no, you did your best. Maybe you did get it wrong, but the loss is his.

Gay at 14?

I'm 14 years old and have a problem. I belong to a swimming club in Hampshire. Before I went there I thought I was gay. Now I'm at the club I've met this really good-looking girl called S . . . . . . She is the woman of my dreams, but I am not sure whether I am still gay. Please could you give me advice? Puzzled-In-Love.

The answer is: some people know for a fact they're gay at 14 and never look at the opposite sex. A lot of straight people have crushes on their own sex at around 14 but remain straight. Anyone like you who is *unsure* at 14 could well be heterosexual. So it's unhelpful to label yourself.

Two loves

I am 11 and I have got a crush on two boys in my class. One of them asked me out and I said no because I was embarrassed and I think the other one likes me but both of them don't know that I like them. What shall I do? From Deeply in Love.

Well, you could always go back to the boy who plucked up courage. If his offer's still open, tell him you've changed your mind. Anyone's allowed to change their mind.

I'm sure he'd be chuffed.

Lives in hope

Last year, I went to a concert with my best friend and his sister (16). Soon after, I asked her out but she refused, though she still wants us to be good friends. Since her brother is my best friend I get to see her all the time. But when I'm with her, I can't express my feelings. How can I say I love her and show my affection without upsetting her? Confused 15-year-old.

This is difficult for you but not impossible. She has said she wants to remain friendly so don't hide your feelings. As long as you don't harass her she can't object to you being nice. If you really love her you won't turn yourself off like a tap. And maybe she'll notice?

Needs more hope

I am a 12-year-old boy and I want to go out with my best friend's 14-year-old sister. She is very pretty but I am just a little squirt and I am a bit shy to ask her out. Please could you give me some advice on what to say? Anon.

I can give you some advice on what to think. If you tell yourself you're a dismal squirt you'll believe it. If you believe you're a squirt, you'll behave like one. Far better to say to yourself, 'I may be younger and she may say no, but I have lots of interesting qualities and I'll give it a go.'

Age-gap 1

Please, Phillip, can you sort out a disagreement I am having with three of my friends? The disagreement is about whether a lad of 21 should go out with a 14–16 year old! I say that it is all right, but my friends say that it is wrong. Please can you tell me who is right or wrong? Gratefully, Mark, Burnley.

You're both right and wrong because it just depends. It depends first on how grown-up the people are and second on what you mean by 'going out with'? For example, it is legal for a girl of 16 to marry a boy of 21 (with her parents' consent). And it's fine for anyone to be 'just friends' with anyone else. But it is against the law for a 21-year-old boy to sleep with a girl who is under the age of 16.

Age-gap 2

I am 13 years old and I am going out with a seven-year-old boy. He's sweet and nice and acts 13. He's good at singing and he gives me lots of stories and songs he's made up. I don't care if I am six years older than him but all my friends think I'm mad to be doing this. My Mum does not know. Please help. Angela (not my real name).

It's great that you share so much and there's nothing wrong with being friends provided *he* can cope. The only trouble is you probably won't have much in common in a year or two's time so please don't break his heart.

Age-gap 3

I'm a 14-year-old girl who has fallen in love with a bus driver who's 20. His name I can't tell you. I go down the town every week and wait until he comes before I go home. I always try to sit near him and I keep phoning him up from school just to hear his voice. The problem is I haven't told my parents. They keep nearly finding out.

For example, every time he beeps his horn – but I just can't tell my parents. Please help me. From a desperate bus driver lover, Dover.

It's not actually illegal to keep some of your feelings a secret you know. As you grow up you will hopefully have more of a *private* life.

Even your parents must expect you to start falling in love one day – if not with Jason Donovan, then with guys in your own home town.

However, I don't suppose Mum and Dad can read your mind. If a bus or lorry driver toots his horn at you, they will only say, 'Yes, she's growing up fast, isn't she?'

I don't think your parents are the problem. I think you are more stuck with loving someone out of your reach. The law says he's too old for you.

It would be different in a couple of years but what you need to do now is open up to someone about the pain of wanting what you can't have. That's the only way to ease the ache in the days ahead, especially if you are thinking of 'waiting for him'.

Silly boyfriend

I have a problem. No one likes my boyfriend and now he is starting to act silly. My best friend said I should get rid of him. If I do I will be upset because I still like him, but he is always silly. What shall I do? Melanie, 10.

It's very important to take people as they are. So you must accept that your boyfriend is sometimes a bit daft *and* that your friends don't think he's wonderful. That's OK. It would be a very silly world where everyone liked everyone and he's your boyfriend, not theirs.

Dumped by Darren

I hope you can help me with my problem. I am 14 and have been going out with a boy called Darren (who is 11 – I know it's silly). We were getting on really well till he didn't meet me one night at the disco. Now he says he's finished with me and going out with someone else. I am so confused and sad and depressed. Anon.

Please don't say it's silly. If you care about someone and they dump you, it always hurts. Whether you are nine or 90, rejection takes away your confidence.

You are telling yourself nobody else will want you. OK – say that. Release the sadness. Soon you will find yourself feeling calmer.

What Darren does is up to him. Maybe he is wonderful. Maybe he's a fool. But if you share this unhappy feeling with those around you, I promise it will change and you will realise Darren is not your judge and jury.

Rejection

I asked a girl out, waiting two days for her to answer. She said yes. I don't think there's words to describe how happy I was.

But the following day, she came up to me and said she 'didn't feel right' and now didn't want to go out with me.

I suppose if she had said 'No' in the first place I wouldn't feel so bad – I would have still felt bad, but not as bad as I now feel.

Ever since she told me I've felt angry at myself but very upset as well. I have actually been thinking of jumping out of my bedroom window, therefore breaking some bones.

Writing to you is the only way I could get it off my chest. What advice would you give me? Anon.

First, you are naturally very cross to be mucked about by someone who changes her mind. She has the right to change her mind, but you have the right to be unhappy about it, so let rip.

Second, it took courage to make your approach to her and it feels terrible to be rejected. However, there is no escape from this feeling. She turned you down. So don't hide the hurt.

Third, you obviously need support. You have this ingenious scheme for getting it by breaking your leg! What you are really saying is that boys can't be looked after when their hearts are broken. They have to break their bodies too. This isn't true.

Fourth, she's made you feel bad enough so don't punish yourself as well. Getting scraped off the tarmac won't help get through to her, because it is your feelings that are damaged, not hers. She may not care what happens to you at all!

Fifth, you are angry because you can see that if you hadn't asked her out you wouldn't feel bad. By this reasoning, none of us would ever risk getting out of bed in the morning.

Lastly, paint her face on your mirror and tell her exactly what you think of her twice a day – from 'I really fancied you' to 'You look like frogspawn!'

Shy love

I am 13 years old. I really like a girl in my class, but every time I try to ask her out I just go all shy and make a fool of myself and she thinks I'm just babyish. What shall I do? Kieron.

You could be less tough on yourself for a start. It is hard at any age to find the courage to ask someone for a date. Rejection is always a possibility and nobody welcomes that. It's even harder when you are doing it for perhaps the first time. So try praising yourself for getting this far.

Second, I'm sure you're wrong about her feeling you're babyish. That's *your* feeling which you are dumping on her. You see, it hasn't crossed your mind that she would *like* to be asked out. And she probably would. And she probably feels nervous too!

So work out what you want to say to her. Practise the words a bit at home. Make sure the right film is playing at the cinema. Choose a time when she's not surrounded by friends or dashing off. Remember to smile. Speak clearly. And who knows? You'll be writing to me next about being too young to go steady.

Loves teacher 1

I've got a nasty problem. You see, my favourite teacher with whom I get along really well is leaving soon. Please can you tell me what to do? It was really nice being his favourite and I will really miss him. Jeanne, aged 10.

Of course you will, even though you can't stop him going. You have to face facts but be kind to yourself.

So don't try to cover up. When people say what's the matter, tell them you're in the dumps. Even tell them why.

Give your nice teacher a pressie the day before he goes and ask whether you can take a photo. Don't give up on the future. After a while, you might find an even *nicer* teacher to work with.

Loves teacher 2

I have a crush on my teacher. A few weeks ago I told him and he started kissing me. He asked if I would like to go out for a meal. What should I say? Yes or no? Katie, aged 13.

No, because all the rules say he shouldn't be touching you. You could break your heart. He could lose his job – or end up in court if things go further.

No, because though it's good to feel loving, it's bad to have guilty secrets. They only hurt your feelings. I think you would be reluctant to tell your parents you were dating this man, wouldn't you?

Yet, crushes are not silly and the feelings are genuinely strong. They show you are learning how to love. The important thing is to enjoy them without getting damaged. That means not staking your life on them. But strangely they always feel worse if you are insecure or unhappy at home. So ask yourself whether you are not covering up some other pain in the process?

Find a good friend to talk to, an aunt, a woman teacher, a school counsellor, someone who won't blab, then let it all out.

Loves teacher 3

I am 13 and in love with my history teacher – he feels the same way about me. I realised this when one history lesson he asked me to stay behind to catch up on some work. Because of the way I felt about him, I agreed to stay behind. When everyone had gone, he came and sat next to me and put his arm around me. I then got up and ran out of the school building. Now every Friday (history lesson day) I pretend to be ill so I don't have to go to school. Please, please help me. From A Very Confused Girl.

You need to unload this on someone. It's too much to deal with by yourself and you can't take every Friday off till you're 16.

Who can you talk to? Is there any adult you trust? What about your best friend? Could you ask her to help you face up to history lessons?

The teacher should not have set you up. If you get your friend to stick to you like glue, he won't be able to repeat the pass. He has a lot to lose, so don't feel helpless. If after all this you still care for him, telling someone reliable makes it bearable. PS – I'm afraid him showing an interest doesn't make it love.

Mad mum

My Mum fancies Phillip Hodson. I honestly can't see why, but she thinks he's absolutely gorgeous. She is driving me crazy talking about him. Anon.

You really must understand that there is *no* accounting for taste. Your mother may seem mad to you, but it's up to her how she feels.

Or are you really feeling threatened because she fancies anyone?

Or is this revenge because she criticises your blokes?

Just remember – the more you moan the more she'll resist. Just like you.

CHAPTER 2

Periods, Breasts and Bras

Mum won't talk?

I have started my periods, but I don't know how to tell my Mum because we don't talk about things like this. How can I tell her? A Phillip Schofield fan.

Having a first period should be a moment of pride for a girl. It's an event that should build up your self-confidence.

So I feel very sad when I hear about Mums (and Dads) who won't or can't talk about this, though I realise even grown-ups can feel shy.

You could lead round to the subject by asking Mum to buy you a small paperback called *Have you started yet?* by Ruth Thomson (published by Piccolo). The title might give her the hint.

Failing this, try speaking to someone you feel comfortable with, who *does* have periods – such as an older sister, aunt or teacher.

Read the book anyway, because it's crammed with helpful advice about dealing with any cramps or backache you might get.

How does it happen?

I haven't started my periods yet and I would like to know what the first signs are. I have also had about three lessons of sex education and haven't told my Mum. Most of what we were told I already knew from friends, but I am getting worried about my periods. An anxious 12-year-old.

Periods can start when you're as young as nine or as old as 17. But, for most girls, it happens between the ages of 11 and 13.

Some time after your breasts start to grow (and the gap can be quite a few weeks), your body prepares to release its first egg.

To look after that egg, a soft landing place is made in the lining of your womb.

But when you don't get pregnant, this lining isn't needed. So your body sheds this lining, and this is what's called a period.

In other words, over several days, a small amount of blood flows out of your vagina (about an egg-cupful).

The first sign you get is a 'show' or small brownish stain in your pants – not enough to colour your outside clothes, so don't worry. You may also have some aches and pains too.

To absorb the blood, you need special pads you can buy from chemists or supermarkets. If you get period pains, a hot-water bottle on the tummy is nice.

There may be a gap of months between your first period and the next. After a while, you will probably settle to a monthly routine. Then you can predict when your next one is due.

If you need to know more, take courage and talk to Mum. She's had periods for years!

Facts of life

We are two very worried twins. We have asked our mother to explain to us the facts of life as we are 13. She will not tell us and neither will our friends. So please could you explain what periods and sex is? New Kids On The Block fans.

I don't think there's room on this page to give you all the facts of life, although at 13 you clearly need to know a lot. So in addition to reading this answer, please get books from your library like

Have you started yet? by Ruth Thomson and *Make it happy* by Jane Cousins.

Sex is the act of making love, usually between a male and female. The penis is placed inside the vagina and the bodies are moved vigorously until pleasure produces orgasm. This causes the sperm to go from the man's to the woman's body to try to fertilise one of her eggs.

Sex is not legal until you are 16 and it's pointless unless you know what you are doing and feel ready to get involved.

Having a period simply means that your body is now releasing a monthly egg and physically preparing your womb to produce a baby. Since you are too young to look after babies yet, and the egg does not meet a male sperm, it gets expelled from the body together with a bit of the womb lining. So for a few days each month, you have a 'bleed' which needs catching in a towel or tampon you can buy from a chemist's.

Bleeding

I have a problem. I can't talk to my Mum and Dad about it, so I wrote to you. It's just that when I go to the toilet blood comes out. So I wondered if you could tell me what to do? Fiona.

I'm glad you did, because you really can write to me about anything.

You don't make it quite clear whether you are starting your periods or have some other type of bleeding. Either way, you need a bit of help.

If it's periods, as I suspect, just take a big breath and tell your Mum. She must be expecting this to happen anyway, so it won't be a dreadful shock.

If it's not periods, don't be scared. The problem is common and usually sorted out by a GP quite easily. Just tell your parents you need to see the doc. So can they make an appointment? When they ask what for, just say it hurts when you go to the loo. When you meet the doc, tell her (or him) everything. Then you can stop worrying.

Period blues

Please help me. I'm really worried. I get very depressed and cry and feel really miserable. Recently, each time has been worse. It doesn't happen very often (about once a month) but when it happens I just go to pieces. It usually lasts for about two or three days each time. Is this normal and do other people have the same problems? Please tell me I'm not alone. Anne, Derbyshire.

You're not alone, Anne. It sounds as though you have pre-menstrual tension (PMT) which affects up to one-third of all women in the country. That's why the feelings are monthly, and last two to three days.

I suggest you prepare for these times. Take things as easily as possible when the mood starts. Give up tea and coffee while you're down (because the caffeine makes things worse). Get some vitamin B6 capsules from the chemist and see if they help. Try to reduce any outside stress – so if you're having rows with your parents, cool it as much as possible. See your GP to get a check-up, anyway.

Period headache?

I am nearly 12 and I suffer terribly with severe headaches. I have been to the doctor's and to the hospital but they will not do anything. What could this be and why don't they do anything? Another thing is that is this a natural thing for a girl my age because I don't just get headaches, I run a temperature of over 102°F and can't move my head. I can't even stand up with such pain. Erika, Somerset.

Headaches are common for girls of your age, Erika, although they still hurt! Your body is going through changes and so are your emotions. Tension in the neck muscles causes headaches; so do rises and falls in hormone levels. Even the way your eyes grow may cause head-pain, so anyone with these symptoms should take an eye test.

However, we don't know why you are also having *fevers.* Please show your parents this answer and get them to request further blood and virus tests for you from the hospital. And make sure the doctors answer two questions: 1 What causes the fever? 2 Why won't they treat it?

Period tease

I have just had my first period. I am 10 years old. I am wearing pads. All of my class knows about it and teases me. I need some advice on how to cope with my problem. Kathy, Scotland.
PS – most of the boys tease me about it because they can't have periods.

Darn right – they feel awkward, 'funny' and left out. They also feel stupid because they don't understand much about periods. But you are quite proud of growing up, so there's no need to get defensive. Smile at them, look happy because things *are* going well. When somebody teases you, run a picture in your mind of that person going bald or sitting on a drawing pin. It helps you cope. When they say 'You're having a period!' reply: 'Yes, I am. Isn't it great!'

Early height

I am 5 feet 8 inches tall and have just turned 12. Most of my friends are 4 feet 8 or 4 feet 10 inches and they laugh because I have long legs. I am very depressed about it. What should I do? A Depressed Tall Person, Newcastle.

You must accept that you have done your growing early. Some people reach average adult height (for British women about 5 feet 7 inches) when they're 11 or 12. It won't be too much time, however, before many of your classmates will have caught up with you.

Meanwhile, please stand up straight and deal with any teasing by looking *down* on your torment-ors. If you cannot think of anything to say in reply, a slow smile from a superior height is always very effective, especially if you carry yourself proudly so others don't feel you are ashamed of being prominent. If you think your whole life has been ruined by your tallness, think again. There will also be *other* reasons why you get upset, which you are now overlooking.

Tampons?

Please could you tell me if it's OK for 12-year-olds to use tampons? Also I read in a book that when you start your periods your breasts stop growing. Is this true? Worried Welsh Girl.

If you are going to use tampons, it's sensible to

ask for the 'mini' size to start with. Both Tampax and Lillets make suitable ones. As for breasts, they *start* growing before your periods come on but certainly continue afterwards (otherwise most women would be flatties, wouldn't they?).

Bad timing?

I am going on holiday with the school and I think my period is due that week. I don't know whether to tell the teacher I am unable to go with them. What should I do? NKOTB fan.

There's no reason to cancel. Just tell your Mum you're worried about this. Make sure you have the right pads or tampons to take with you. Discuss things with a teacher if you need. But remember that periods don't stop you from moving about. You can go dancing all night if you want. So have a good time.

Missing period 1

Please help. I am 14 years old and I have not had my period for three months and I can't be pregnant because I have not had an affair with anybody. I'm too embarrassed to see my doctor. What can I do? Anon.

Periods can be irregular for lots of reasons, so please stop worrying about being pregnant. You're not.

This being so, there should be no difficulty about seeing your doctor to get the whole thing sorted out.

She (or he) will probably tell you it's a weight/ hormone problem and give you treatment.

But remember, if you've only just started, your

second period can take some weeks to arrive anyway.

Missing period   2

My period is late. I had my first period in the last week of August. I have not yet had another. I am worried that there is something wrong with me. Please help. K., Belfast.

Unless you've lost weight, there's absolutely nothing to worry about. It's very common to go for six to nine months between the first and your next period. However, if you've been crash-dieting, please see the doc.

Needs a bra?   1

I think I need a bra but I'm not sure how to ask my Mum for one. I think if I ask her she will laugh and say I'm being silly. From a Kylie and Jason fan.

Then get your argument ready. Tell her that you may not be big-chested, but other reasons exist for wearing bras. Such as wanting to look like the other girls. Such as not being teased because you haven't got one. Such as wanting one because you want one (where's the harm, anyway?).

My challenge to you is this. If you're grown up enough to wear a woman's clothes, you've got to be grown up enough to argue and reason to get them. So take the risk and fight your corner. Mum will have to give in one day, won't she?

Needs a bra?   2

I am 12 years old and in my first year of secondary school. At my last school, the nurse told us we should

*start wearing a bra as soon as possible. My Mum bought
me a bra and I've tried to wear it and it's comfortable at
first, but then it starts getting itchy and I take it off. I
told my Mum this but she just said, 'It's the most
comfortable one available so you'd better get used to
wearing it!' But I can't. Then a friend said I should
wait till I'm older before I wear it. Now I don't know
what to do. Brenda, Essex.*

The most important information is missing. You
don't tell me the *size* of this problem.

If your boobs are big, then a bra will give you the
necessary support. However, the fact is that some
women go right through life quite happily never
wearing or needing to buy a bra.

I guess you are at a stage where your chest is also
very sensitive to the slightest touch from tight
clothing. Since this irritability will lessen as you
develop, perhaps it would be best to wait a bit
longer.

Needs a bra? 3

*Please help me. I am 13. I have not started my periods
but I have pubic hair under my arms and down below
and I have a small bust (size 30 inches). However, my
Mum won't let me wear a bra because she said I am
only allowed to wear one when I have started my
periods. All the other girls in my class wear one.
Sometimes, I get a bit jealous but when I do any
running my bust wobbles; sometimes I have to stop
because it hurts and feels tender. A Worried 13-year-old
Girl.*

Remind your Mum that breasts start before
periods so her rule does sound a little strange. It
also makes you feel like the odd one out at school

when you need to belong. If she's worried about the cost, tell her you'll help save up the money. But don't panic. From what you've said, your periods are due jolly soon.

Nipples

Please help me, Phillip. The problem is my breasts are growing but the nipples aren't. Sometimes when I wake up, one of my nipples has got little lumps on and the other hasn't. It doesn't hurt and they soon disappear. Please help because I am really scared. Fiona, a Fast Forward *fan, aged 13.*

I am really glad to be able to tell you that everything is normal, Fiona. These little bumps only appear when you get a bit chilly or excited. (Maybe you have really interesting dreams!)

One female breast is never truly identical to the other. It may be larger or smaller, lean to left or right or have slightly different skin. It may also respond more to cold or warmth.

Nipples, too, differ. Some people have pointy ones; others have 'inverted' ones which only show up when someone gives you a thrill or chucks a bucket of water over your T-shirt. Some people even have more than one set of nipples, but I think that's quite enough breast talk for now.

Big breasts at nine

Please help. My breasts are big. Everybody stares and laughs at me. I'm the only girl in my class that wears a bra (I'm nearly nine). Is there something wrong with me? Please answer – I am deeply distressed. Anon.

It's really tough to get teased for being absolutely

normal. But some girls do start their periods at the age of eight or nine. To make it more difficult, breasts start to grow even before you get your periods.

Tell yourself there are pluses and minuses. First, you are well. You are maturing before the rest. You can be sure of having a figure. You will not be disturbed by your body as a teenager (since you are going through the changes now).

On the other hand, it is inevitable that some people will make jokes, *so be prepared for this.* Say 'I've heard it all before', over and over to yourself.

Also tell yourself that people who tease are *always anxious.* In your case, they are secretly envious of what you've got and they want.

Wants big breasts

I'm very worried because I've only got small breasts and my friends have big breasts. Is it normal or is there something wrong with me? A worried and scared girl, aged 13.

It's normal. I know you want to be the same as all your friends, but if you look around you'll notice the differences.

For instance, you all take various shoe sizes. You all have different sorts of noses. You all have different shapes of legs, ankles, ears, heads, eyes and mouths. Some belly buttons go in. Some stick out. Some hands are big; some small.

It's the same with breasts. Sizes vary from as little as about 30 inches to as much as 40 inches or more when women are fully grown. But growth is not usually complete until you reach at least the age of 16 or more, so please don't panic.

Thoughts about boys

*I have loads of worries and problems, not anyone's fault.
I just, well, can't stop my thoughts coming. I have a sort
of obsession about babies. I am always writing down
names of babies (especially girls) and thinking about
how they are made. I also think about boys and sex and
bras. I suppose I am too young but I can't stop myself.
Please tell me what to do. Love, Sam (not my real
name). I am 13.
PS – I am sending you a 5p bribe to answer this.*

You sound totally normal to me. This is the age
when you start to wonder about becoming a
woman, including (one day) possibly a mum. I
should talk to someone you can trust about your
worries without apologising for having them. We
are all entitled to be confused! It might be a good
idea to read some books about 'boys and sex and
bras' (e.g. *Make it happy* by Jane Cousins, Penguin
Books).
PS – Thanks for the bribe, but it won't work and
I'm sending it back.

CHAPTER 3

Other bodily problems

Won't want baby

I really hope you can answer my question: Why can't boys have babies? I like babies but don't like how they come. I want boys to have them. It can't be impossible, because nothing's impossible. Also, if you have a healthy baby, what must you eat and drink? Anon.

Boys can't have babies because their bodies are the wrong shape inside. They can't make a nest for the egg, they can't supply food for it and they cannot move their bones to allow space for a birth.

It's not true that everything is possible, though some scientists believe that if a woman donated a fertilised egg a man could carry a baby in his body for a couple of months.

I hear *you* saying you are a bit afraid of giving birth. Well, it doesn't have to happen *unless* you want it to. And it doesn't have to happen *until* you want it to.

By the time you are ready to have children of your own (or not), lots of people will have helped you come to terms with these feelings.

PS – pregnant mums can eat more or less what they want, but shouldn't smoke or drink alcohol.

Has leukaemia

I have been suffering from leukaemia, a bone-marrow disease, for a long time now. Even though it's been hard, I have come to terms with this. But my family don't give me the support I need.

Don't get me wrong. I love my Mum and Dad very much, but they don't like me to talk about my illness. I need someone to talk to. I need them to help me. They always argue and shout when they talk and I just wish

I could die now and leave them. I'm sure they would be happier. Please help. Sad Child.

Your parents probably feel guilty because you are ill and angry because they cannot make you well. They are afraid to face these feelings, so their instinct is to avoid discussing your illness.

You, on the other hand, very much need to talk about your fears and worries for the future. To help you cope. And to make you better. Leukaemia is often beaten *because* someone feels self-confident about fighting it.

Try to find someone in your family you could say this to – aunt, uncle, grandparent – and ask them to explain to your parents that if they could just let you express your anxiety about your health, and your bad luck, and how tired you often feel, you'd be ever so much happier, and maybe healthier. If there's no one in the family, ask your doctor to tell them. And I promise they will also benefit from getting things off their chests.

Has diabetes

I have diabetes. I've had this for a long time – in fact, it will be ten years this year. I am coping quite well, but my problem is that most other people don't know what diabetes is and when I try to tell them I don't think they understand that it matters. I shall have diabetes for the rest of my life. And famous people don't do anything about it either. They always raise money for cancer, etc. I have injections every day and very big lumps on the sides of my legs which are embarrassing. I got this illness when I was two and a half. Please support me. Anon.

OK – diabetes is of two main kinds and basically means your body cannot control levels of sugar in your blood. You have what's called Type 1 where you need to inject insulin to keep things in balance. And if you don't inject, you can start to feel very ill. So I know there's lots of worry and sheer inconvenience in your life. But there are half a million diabetics in this country – you're not alone – and treatment is developing all the time. The good news is that diabetes can usually be controlled, unlike some forms of cancer. And you can help protect yourself – ask your doctor about getting a medical bracelet to wear to alert people to your condition if you are ever taken ill.

Smelly body

We are two friends with a problem. There is a girl in our class we are really good friends with, but the problem is she smells badly of BO. Everyone talks about her behind her back. We would like to do something without hurting her feelings. What should we do? From two Brossettes.

BO – the dreaded Body Odour (from stale sweat and unwashed shirts) which apparently we mustn't talk about. Nutmegs! Just take her to one side and tell her. She now needs to change her blouse daily, avoid non-cotton fabrics and use a deodorant. Puberty has firmly struck and her body is producing pongy stuff from her *apocrine* sweat glands. Before puberty, children smell sweet; afterwards, nobody does unless they clean up every day. If it helps, show her this answer but stress the bit about being really fond of her.

Eyebags

When I was nine, I started to form bags under my eyes. After one night of short sleep, my bags increase by up to

*four millimetres and take two weeks to disappear. I am
ashamed to look at other people and I am desperate.*

*Please, please, please, please, please, please could you
help?*

*I have been to the doctor seven or eight times, but she
says I should just go to bed earlier. I thought doctors
were supposed to help people, not send them back home if
there was something wrong? Anon.*

Your problem isn't bags – they happen because all
this worry about your life and appearance is
making you too tense to sleep properly. Anyone
gets bags when the muscles under their eyes get
tired! A doctor cannot help you since you are not
ill. Although a smart doctor would see what's
really going on.

Your real problem is about feeling not-OK. You
project this onto your poor, innocent eyes. You are
very sensitive and cannot bear any criticism. You
naturally want to look perfect like the rest of us.
But with you it is because you believe it would
solve all your other problems too, which the rest of
us know it won't.

You are certain the world is itching to reject you.
Why?

Excess sweat

*Please could you put me out of my embarrassing
situation? It is that I sweat a lot. It's not only smelly at
times, but it also seeps through all my clothes. I do use
an antiperspirant deodorant and I also wash under my
arms. The deodorant does take the smell away but the
seeping continues. Please print this letter as I'm sure
other girls have this problem. Bros fan, West Sussex.*

Of course it's not only girls who worry. The problem can affect anyone.

Worse still, worrying about it can actually make you sweat *more* because anxiety stimulates your sweat glands.

Let's agree that sweating is normal. You get rid of up to 2 litres of water every day from your body, much of it by sweating. It happens when you get tense and it happens in order to cool down your skin.

If you are very fat or drink too much tea, coffee and Coke containing caffeine you will sweat more. So deal with this yourself by eating and drinking less.

If you wear plastic or nylon clothes, your sweat will make more mess, so try to get cotton underwear and shirts.

If the problem is really big (and I mean ginormous) see your doc, because they have remedies that help. They also need to check you out.

But so long as you wash, and change your underclothes *daily*, the smell should offend no one. Fresh sweat is actually a turn-on. (It's only 24 hours later that we begin to wonder who's died!)

Flea bites

I am a 10-year-old boy (nearly). For a few weeks I have had all these lumps coming out from my skin. I think they are bites. I've got about 15. I've tried washing my bed, washing my pyjamas and taking my bears out of my bed. They itch like mad but I don't scratch them. I've got some cream from the doctor but it doesn't do anything. Help, before I'm eaten alive. Anon.

I also bet you've got a cat or some pet in the house

who's probably harbouring fleas. (Sorry if this
sounds insulting, Moggy.)

First, take a trip to the vet for flea pills, flea
spray, a flea comb and a flea collar. (No, you put
this on the cat, not yourself.)

Repeat the process of cleaning your bed, bears
and clothes but this time with the spray. Keep the
cat out of your bedroom for a couple of weeks and
you should soon be OK.

Spots' spot

*I have a lot of spots and I'm fed up with squeezing them
and wasting my money on spot stuff which doesn't work.
Even my best friend calls me 'beanface'. Anon.*

Most adults don't understand how miserable you
feel when your face is patrolled by acne spots.
They've forgotten what it is like, or they wouldn't
make such silly jokes about them. Nor would they
say: 'Don't worry. They'll definitely be gone by the
time you're 26!'

So here's the truth. Acne is normal for 70 per
cent of teenagers. It does not mean you're dirty –
in fact, too much washing can make things worse.
The colour in blackheads is skin pigment, not
muck.

The good news is that 75 per cent of acne cases
will improve after eight weeks, but you do have to
follow these rules:

First, accept that no rapid cure is available. I'll
repeat that in case you didn't get the point. *Acne
cannot be cleared up overnight.* Second, decide
whether your problem is mild or severe (tricky, I
realise). If things aren't too bad, go to the chemist
and buy a recommended product.

Third, use the product properly for two solid months. It takes that long to work.

Fourth, if you have a great army of spots, see your doctor because he or she can try other drugs on you.

Fifth, don't squeeze spots. They are just as likely to explode inwards causing more infection and fingers are always filthy.

Sixth, sex does not cause spots or every adult would be covered in the things.

Seventh, tell yourself that people notice your spots less than you do because you value your looks more than they do.

Last, remember that nobody is a perfect '10' anyway.

Moles galore

I have a lot of moles. My friends, the few I have, make fun of them and call me names like ADRIAN MOLE. It is really upsetting me and I am becoming self-conscious of them. It is not as if you can use spot cream and they will go away. Please help. Gerard.

Since (most) moles are normal, natural skin markings we've all got them and we have to live with them. Tell yourself they are not shameful, so if someone teases you about them he is really pretty stupid. And if you made more friends anyway, it wouldn't seem half so lonely and difficult.

Lip-picker

I have a problem which concerns my lips. The cold weather dries the skin making it flaky. Then I do the stupid thing and pick the skin off. It is painful and leaves sores. What should I do? Tessa, 16.

Do what I have to do, Tessa – buy a 99p tube of lipsalve from any chemist's (brand names include Lipsyl and Labello). Apply to your lips every cold morning after brushing your teeth. Use it again when you go out in the afternoon. Then the wind won't damage your skin, which won't flake, which won't irritate you, which won't make you nibble it bloody.

Undersized body

Please could you help me? I am sure I have got a growing problem. I am 14 and the smallest third year. Most of the first years are bigger than me.

My Mum said I should wait until I am 15, then she will take me to the doctor.

But I can't see why I can't go now. Everyone thinks I am 12 years old. And my sister who is eight is bigger than me. I don't want to be small all my life. Anon.

We all grow at different rates. Somebody has to be the smallest in the class and if your parents are short, then it's likely you will be too.

However, it's also possible you *do* have a growth problem. If so, it's essential to get help at once.

Tell your Mum doctors can do nothing once you have reached a 'grown-up' age. She should write to the Child Growth Foundation, 2 Mayfield Avenue, Chiswick, London W4 1PW to get the full facts.

Wet bed

I am 10 years old and I feel as if I am a baby as I still wet the bed. I have a plastic sheet on my bed. Please can you help me – I sometimes think I am still a baby and not a girl? Yours hopefully, X.

The first point to realise is that this is not your fault. Fifteen per cent of five-year-olds wet the bed; 5 per cent of ten-year-olds do it and between 1 and 12 per cent of teenagers and adults do it.

SEVENTY-FIVE PER CENT OF CHILDREN DO IT, IF BOTH THEIR PARENTS USED TO SUFFER WITH THE PROBLEM WHEN THEY WERE YOUNG.

Bed-wetting (inability to control the bladder while sleeping) is largely an inherited problem. Your brain cannot learn as quickly or as easily how to control your bladder muscle as can the brains of other children. It just takes longer.

REMEMBER: WE ALL WET THE BED (OR OUR NAPPIES) WHEN WE ARE BABIES AND WE ALL HAVE TO LEARN BLADDER CONTROL.

It is helpful to bear in mind that fresh urine is *not* dirty but sterile and is actually used to clean wounds when other materials are unavailable.

Half the fuss and trouble with bed-wetting arises because parents: 1 think you are being careless when you are not; and 2 they get extra work to do.

Treatment

1 See your GP – because your bed-wetting just might be caused by some sort of infection and this needs to be checked.

2 Drink less after 6 pm. Drink normally during the day.

3 If you go to the loo more often than every three to four hours, practise waiting another half an hour or so. This helps your bladder get used to *less* frequent urination.

4 Change your own sheets and organise the

washing of your own bedclothes. This puts you firmly in charge of the problem, cuts down the cause of irritation for others and means that the rest of the family doesn't need to interfere in your personal hygiene.

5 There are several 'bell and pad' type devices that can train you to wake up when you need to pee. Ask your GP about getting one of these systems.

6 After giving these methods a fair chance, return to your doctor if you still need help. There are some drugs that might eventually be tried.

Is it dandruff?

I have a hair problem. I have little bits of white flakes coming out of my hair when I comb it. It isn't dandruff. I wash my hair with an anti-dandruff shampoo but next day the white flakes are back again. Can you help? Brian, aged 14.

It doesn't matter what you call it, but these little white flakes *are* particles of dead skin falling from your scalp. In fact, you are probably using *too* much of the special shampoo thus irritating your skin. Instead, try a mild 'frequent wash' shampoo, plus the odd treatment once a fortnight from the strong stuff. See your doctor for a check-up too.

Leg shaving?

I am 11½ years old and everyone at school – well, all my friends – have shaved their legs and they said why don't you do it? I said no, because it's silly. And my friends called me a baby, so I did shave my legs. I told my Mum and she went mad. Then she said not to do it again. I felt so embarrassed. I ran upstairs and didn't show my face. What will I do? Julie.

PS Please print my letter because I need your help and I think your advice page is good and I think you should make it bigger.

I think everyone is getting things out of proportion – you, your friends and even your Mum. We are talking about a few hairs on your legs not nuclear war.

Everyone's entitled to their view. If your mates feel grown up with smooth legs, fine. If you think it's a waste of time, stick to your guns, though tell the others you can sort of see why they want to do it.

As for your Mum, she clearly does not feel too comfortable with your looming teenage. Tell her shaving doesn't do any damage; nor will it mean the hairs grow back tougher. It's just a bore to have to keep doing it. So if she goes on about it, ask her . . . well . . . to keep her hair on!

Bearded girl?

Please help. I am only 14 years old and it looks as though I am growing a beard. I get picked on a lot at school and they call me 'beardy'. I am very conscious of it. The doctor said that my male hormone level was high and not to shave it as it would makes things worse. I am worried that it will affect my exams, and my chance of having a boyfriend.

The trouble with shaving is *not* that it strengthens hair – that's a myth. But once you start, you have to carry on, otherwise the stubble is prickly. (You can get a ladies' razor from the chemist.)

Some dark-haired girls are very hairy even though their bodies work perfectly. You could ask your Mum whether you can get some help from a

beautician. There are dyes and bleaches, camou-
flage make-up or even treatments like electrolysis
if it bothers you enough.

Warty Welsh girl

*The problem is my warts. I have got 12 of them and they
are all quite big. I have tried everything to cure them but
they won't go. Please give me some help as they look
really ugly. Thanks. A Warty Welsh Girl, aged 10.*

Well, you haven't tried going to your doctor
because he or she could help you get rid of them
quite quickly. Warts are caused by a little bug
called a virus. Cutting and digging won't help. The
virus burrows deeper into your skin. You need to
get the whole thing destroyed in one go. To do
this, your GP can give you an anaesthetic, then
either freeze or burn the warts painlessly off.

Weight on mind

*I have a problem. I am 10 years old and weigh 6½
stone. I keep thinking I am overweight and fat. My
Mum, sister and friends say I'm not, but I think they
are just being nice. I need help and am really worried.
From a Very Worried Person.*

OK, just go to the doctor and ask for the truth. I
think you'll find the GP agrees with your Mum,
but why not check it out for yourself?

Blushing

*I have got a problem which is getting me down. When I
see someone I know down the street my face goes bright
red for no reason. Or if a teacher asks me to read in the*

class or do something in front of anyone I still go red. I can feel my face burning up which makes me even more embarrassed knowing that I'm red. Please help. Julie, Blackpool.

Well, you've proved that your blush system is working normally! We've all got this ability to go red when we feel alarmed. It means the blood is pumped closer to the skin surface. This helps get rid of the extra heat caused by making the heart race.

Now, the nitty-gritty is this. Your body is not to blame, because there *is* a reason for the fiery complexion. Becoming over-alarmed causes the problem. You get alarmed because you lack confidence and don't know what to do when given public attention.

The basic answer is to tell yourself you are not stupid. If you keep slow regular control of your breathing you won't panic. If you give up avoiding people and situations, you won't add to your anxiety. And if you give yourself permission to be sometimes lost for words, the pressure will come down even more.

Do you really have to be perfect? No. Try being 'good enough' instead.

How to sleep

I find it very hard at night to get to sleep, especially on Sundays. I cannot seem to switch off. I don't know why but I keep getting a temptation to think about lots of things and although I'm tired my mind won't let me go to sleep. Please tell me why this happens? Pia, Scotland.

In our brains, we have a 'body-clock' which

controls sleep rhythm. Alas, it is set to a 25-hour cycle, so we always want to stay up a bit later at night, and get up later in the morning. Weekends are a special problem if you have a lie-in on a Saturday. When it's time for bed on Sunday, you won't feel drowsy. And the remedy is – don't have lie-ins!

You will also upset your body-clock if you don't eat proper regular meals and if you don't exercise. So don't complain if you can't sleep on a diet of Yorkie bars and Coke.

As for switching off, Pia, you need to make your lists of 'Things To Do Tomorrow' well before bedtime. Bed is for sleeping, not for plotting or worrying. Bear in mind you need to wind down before you can sleep. So it's no use going straight from homework, or TV, to bed. Sit and chat first, get warm, grow floppy. And if you've got real problems or worries, discuss them at 8.30 in the morning with people who can do something about them.

You can help release the sleep hormone (serotonin) if a couple of hours before bedtime you eat a mix of carbohydrate and fat. So a supper of baked potato with cheese, or cereal with milk and banana is recommended. (No, not as an extra meal – instead of your normal scoff.)

Happy dream

Could you please answer a question I have about dreams? I am a disabled teenager (born with spina bifida). Whenever I have a dream which involves myself, 99 per cent of the time I am able-bodied in the dream. Could you please tell me why this is? Although in real life it would be very nice to be able-bodied, it does not worry me being disabled. Laura.

Yes, it's simple really, Laura. When you dream, the picture of yourself is really about the 'inner' you, not your body. The good news is that you see yourself as a whole person – your imagination is whole, your feelings are whole, your spirit is whole. As a person, Laura feels complete when she dreams and that's great!

CHAPTER 4

My bad habits

Compelled to be mean

*My secret is that I am very mean. I hate having to buy
people presents and I always try and get out of it by
telling myself 'Oh, I don't expect they want anything
anyway' or 'They've got everything they need – I'll just
get some cheap, jokey little thing.'*

*And something else – if I'm really honest, I'm not just
mean about money. I don't like saying 'Well done' to my
friends or thinking of nice treats for them. Can someone
learn not to be mean? Craig.*

Of course, but you have to realise why you behave
like Scrooge in the first place. It's not that you're
evil, but you probably have been treated
ungenerously by others – deprived of presents and
praise. Maybe the grown-ups in your life really
disapprove of any show gestures – maybe they are
puritans. Now, you seem trapped – if you do
reward someone, you fear feeling silly or sad. It
will remind you of what you have never had. But
there is a way out, since life is all about learning.
Start giving yourself some treats, thinking you
deserve more fun and experiment slowly by being
just a little less tight-fisted with others. They usually won't take advantage of you if you're nice –
they'll probably only be nicer back.

Anxious mum

*Would you please give my son a ring – he still sucks his
thumb even though he will be 14 years old shortly. He's
worse now than when he was a baby.*

*He is driving us all mad because as soon as he sits
down to watch television in goes his thumb and with the
other hand he twiddles his hair.*

We have tried all sorts to make him stop, told him big

boys don't suck their thumbs and even bought him a dummy (which he threw away immediately). We are now desperate for an instant cure. As a last resort would you try talking to him for us? Anon.

This is your problem. You should do a relaxation exercise. We all grow up at different rates and parts of us grow up faster than others. Your son won't be thumb-sucking at 25 – but it could be that he will carry on getting comfort like this so long as his Mum makes fun of his need to feel secure. I prescribe more cuddles and less irritation from you – remember, parts of him are adult and parts are very child-like – he's not a grown-up.

Nail-biter

How can I stop biting my nails? I know they look really horrible. I've tried that Stop n' Grow but I have got used to the taste so that isn't helping me much now. Trouble is, I like chewing 'em. Gayle.

Don't get too worked up about this. After all, the planet isn't going to die just because you nibble your fingers. But if you want to break the habit, here are six suggestions:

1 The chemist can help with other products like Nil Nite, Mavala, etc., costing from £1.50 to £3.50.
2 Try nail hardeners (basically varnish) or false nails. The latter can be fused on by a beautician or you can glue them yourself, then cut them to shape. They are difficult, not to say unrewarding, to chew. Can be worn by either sex.
3 Wear gloves in bed, even if your problem turns into 'I chew gloves in bed', to which the answer is 'So what?'

4 Get a manicure set. Your own vanity is a powerful tool. Making your hands look nice becomes addictive.

5 Play with worry beads – you can make your own – and they will keep nervous hands occupied while you watch TV.

6 Agree to bite your nails only at 1 pm and 6 pm every day.

As soon as you impose a routine on the habit, you find it becomes tedious.

Finally, research shows that getting engaged works wonders, since you may want to display a ring on prettier fingers; but this may seem like going too far!

Wants to smoke

I have the problem of getting these funny feelings that I need a cigarette. I am aged 11 and my brother smokes at 15 years old. When he's out, I go in his bedroom, through all his drawers, looking for a cigarette but I haven't found one yet. Why does this happen and can you help me? From a desperate Cigarette Wanter.

Two reasons why this might happen. First, if lots of people in your house smoke, you may be getting a craving because you swallow their second-hand smoke. It's much more fun to say 'Can I have some fresh air in here, please?' than turn yourself into another chimney. Leave the room if they won't stop. Secondly, I think you are also jealous of your older brother and you mistakenly believe if you copy his behaviour you will get treated like a grown-up. Sorry – it won't happen. If you start to smoke, you will remain the junior child but this time with a bad cough and a pocket-money problem.

Stealing addict

I am 11 coming on 12. I am small but I have a big problem. My brother has a paper round and every Friday he collects money. He keeps the bag under the stairs. I take money from the bag to spend in the town. I can't stop even if I try. I don't get pocket money and I need money. I want to stop. Will you help me? Anon.

We all need some cash, but stealing it is not only wrong but risky. One day soon, your brother is going to find out and then you will be in trouble *and* skint. Ask your parents if you can have some pocket money. If they can't or won't supply it, ask if you can earn any money around the house or get yourself a paper round like your brother.

Food junky

I am writing to you in a state of aggression and depression. I am 15, in the last year of my GCSEs. Some months ago, weighing 10 stones 4 pounds and standing 5 feet 8 inches, I went on a diet. After a month and a half, I had lost one stone and didn't stop dieting. I am now 8 stones 8 pounds. I don't eat breakfast, just have a drink, then during the day at school I get two drinks of hot chocolate from the machine we have. When I get home, I usually go and eat compulsively and then, feeling guilty, vomit my food. I do this after supper too. I have been following this regular routine for almost two months.

I am writing because I frequently get moody and depressed and filled with aggression – I never take it out on anybody. Can you help? I don't want to live this way for ever. Anon.

You suffer from bulimia – a common eating disorder caused by fear of being fat – you binge and then you purge. You are actually making these bad moods by semi-starving yourself: hunger leads to feeling over-hyped, and after being sick you get a rush of blood – so the aggression/depression is mainly physical. Being sick so often is *dangerous* – the powerful stomach acid can damage your gullet and make you bleed inside. It can also dissolve your teeth and seriously impair your digestive system. I understand your wish not to get fat again, but there is another way to manage the food supply. (Bingeing is more likely to make you over-weight in the end.) Just please eat breakfast – banana, muesli, skimmed milk and *keep it down.* Your blood sugar will go up and you won't feel hungry. Eat four to five small meals a day – an apple at break and so on. That way your stomach will shrink (which it can't if you binge), you won't get hunger pangs and you won't need to gorge or vomit.

Addicted

I am only 11 years old and am addicted to alcohol. I started drinking when I was nine. I only started through a sip of my Mum's wine. It has come to sneaking drink when my Mum is out. What should I do? Anon.

I doubt that you are addicted to alcohol yet. I would guess you are stuck in the daredevil habit of swigging some of Mum's booze when you're alone. It sounds as though you are bored as well as bothered. Don't spend so much time away from your friends. And when you get the urge to filch a drink, make yourself count out loud to a hundred first. Do it slowly. Then challenge yourself *not* to open the bottle at all. (It can eventually be more exciting to stay in charge of yourself than to break the rules.)

Pill thief

I have a serious problem. I have been taking my Mum and Dad's pills and I am now addicted to them. Please, please can you try to help me to stop? I started when I was about seven. PLEASE CAN YOU HELP ME?
From a really troubled schoolgirl.

From what you say, I guess these are likely to be sleeping pills or tranquillisers such as Valium or Librium. Chemically, sleeping pills and tranquillizers are nearly identical, though a lot of people don't realise they may be hooked on tranquillizers when they simply 'take a pill to go to sleep'. Yes, you can get very addicted to these and must be careful how you come off. If you're not prepared to tell your doctor, start to reduce the dose gradually, taking three-quarters of a tablet in the first week, half a tablet in the second, and keep reducing slowly over several weeks. Be prepared for some withdrawal symptoms – panics, jumpiness, bad dreams – for some weeks after that. You have to teach your brain to function without pills – and it's likely to protest. There are also lots of organisations that can help you in confidence – for instance, Release on 071-603 8654.

Doesn't want to smoke

Please help me – I am 10 years old and my friends and I have started to smoke. I want to stop. What do I do? I don't want to die. Phillip Schofield fan.

When you stop smoking, the worst effect is a kind

of flu-feeling in the head. It may last for a couple of weeks. So it's quite easy to become a non-smoker by staying away from ciggies.

The real test is finding something else to do with your time and not responding to smokers who tease you.

So ask your parents to get a project going with you. And tell any teasers smoking is *not* grown-up. Most adults don't smoke, so who's really being childish?

Still smokes

I smoke and I'm 12 years old. I started when I was six. I've tried to stop but I can't. My brother started me off. All my mates smoke so it's harder for me. I've tried your advice before. It didn't work. Could you give me more advice, please? My Mum don't know I do it. Help! Claire.

OK, toughie, so you're telling me you have no control over your life. This is false but you feel it to be true.

All smokers are actually drug addicts. Nicotine is the culprit. But the difficulties of giving up smoking have often been exaggerated.

So let's be clear that your *real* problems are as follows. You are short on self-confidence. You worry about being different from your mates. And you are afraid of change.

I won't add that smoking costs £25,000 for a shortened life-span spent coughing. Nor that 100,000 people die every year because of it. These cut no ice.

I just challenge you to prove me wrong. Have a 'mild cold' by stopping. You can be free in two weeks if you want. But it does mean you have to be firm with yourself and your friends – but why should they ruin your health for you?

Steals cigarettes

I've got a problem I don't know how to solve. I smoke. I've tried to stop but it's no use. I am 11 years old and I've been smoking for a year. No one knows I do it so please don't give my name.

I am under the age for buying ciggies but I find them somehow.

I started in April 1988. My Dad asked me to go and fetch his ciggies from our car and I just lit one up and I've been doing it ever since. Nicking them from my Dad when nobody is looking. I smoke round the back of our house by a bench.

My health depends on you – please give me some tips before it's too late.

The first thing to say is what a handicap any child has when parents smoke. Naturally, you want to be like them and grow up doing what they do. So I don't think it's entirely your fault you're smoking.

If you have a good relationship with your family, why not confess your problem and ask them for help – maybe you could all give up smoking together?

However, I can't help noticing you are only 11 and seem to want to grow up awfully fast, which must mean it's not very comfortable for you to be your proper age. Even so, there are other ways to feel more important and confident – especially spending more time making friends. Sneaking round the back of the house for a quick drag is hardly that fascinating in fact.

As I've said before, getting rid of the physical craving will only take a couple of weeks, then have a supply of chewing gum to munch whenever you want to stick something in your mouth to help with the mental withdrawal.

Thumb sucker

I have a problem – it is sucking my thumb. I've sucked my thumb since I was two and I cannot stop. I hope you print this letter because I know I'm not the only one. I am now 13 and my teeth are coming forward, so please give me some advice before I have really bucked teeth. From Tracey, Lancashire.

You're right, this is a common problem. However, there's nothing wrong with thumb-sucking itself. People do it as a comforter. The real trouble is it ruins your teeth as you pull them forward.

Therefore I'd suggest using a substitute. You could try sugar-free chewing gum, which dentists now believe is excellent for your teeth and gums. You could make yourself a pleasant, private cuddle cloth to suck at night.

But if you do find your thumb in your mouth, change position and push your teeth from the front with your thumb-pad. If you suck in that position, some of the damage will gradually be undone.

And remember – the alternative is braces!

Cheeks parents

My problem is that I can't stop being cheeky to my Mum and Dad. Another thing is that I can't stop sucking my thumb. JD fan.

Possibly your two problems are related. Maybe you suck your thumb for comfort and answer back to feel more important. Both suggest you could do with extra, not less, attention. Why not put it to Mum and Dad that you'll stop being cheeky if they'll treat you as more of a grown-up? No, I don't just mean increase your pocket money. I mean let you stay up a bit later and spend additional time on family activities – go skating, watch movies, make trips. If thumb-sucking really bugs you, ask people to let you know when you do it and tell them what's on your mind instead. That's the way to retrain a habit.

CHAPTER 5

About death and sadness

Living with dying

I'm a 13-year-old girl with terminal cancer who's been in and out of hospital since being nine. I return to school occasionally when I'm well enough. The trouble is that my classmates talk to me as if I'm a freak, especially the girls.

Most of the time I'm in a lot of pain and when I lay in bed I think to myself why won't the doctors let me die? What's the point of keeping me alive when I know I'm going to die soon? I feel so depressed, most of my days are spent crying.

When my mother's friend knew how low I was feeling all she could say was that there are other children who are in the same boat as me but they're not wishing they were dead. In other words, I should pull myself together. But why has this happened to me? Why am I being punished? Why couldn't it have happened to someone else who's done evil in this world?

I'm so angry with God when I see my father's face when he knows I'm in pain. The tears pour down his face. Why should God make him suffer too? I have a friend from school, John, who's precious to me. Wherever I am he's always there. He visits me in hospital, he comes to my home, he even brings me little gifts to cheer me up when I'm feeling down but most of all he listens to what I've got to say which is the kindest thing anyone could do. If ever there's a time when he needs me, I will repay all his kindness. I love that boy. Trisha.

I'd glad you can share your sadness with me. It must seem impossible to bear what is happening to you and there is no obvious sense to it. You cannot 'deserve' this illness; you must feel real fury. Who the hell chose you? No one.

The worst of it, *apart from the pain*, is having to live your whole life so quickly, coming into contact with people who cannot react properly. People are afraid of death, so they tune out or get tough. We all die, and it's rarely easy – but we usually are better able to pace things than you can.

Concentrate on the important bits – loving your Dad, bless him; and John. One advantage is you can say *anything* you like, telling them how much you care for them – and we all send you a hug.

Now so cross

My mother died in February of last year. I blamed Dad for Mum's death at first but it was no one's fault (she had cancer). Dad and me used to row a lot just after her death about stupid things – e.g. whether I could go into town, what we would have to eat, etc. I suppose he was just under a lot of pressure. We have now just moved from a four-bedroomed house to a two-bedroomed flat. We have rowed about practically everything over the flat, colour of carpets and curtains and where should everything go. In your column, could you say something to try and stop children from arguing and rowing with their parents like this? Anon.

No, I'm afraid I couldn't. There are times when we really *need* to row and clear the air, especially when tragedy strikes as it has you and your Dad.

You see, it's natural to be angry with someone for dying. You and Dad have been able to let some of this steam off at each other. He didn't want you to go into town in case he lost another member of his family. You rowed about what to eat because I imagine cooking used to be Mum's job. You were distressed to be reminded of losing her services too. Her death made you live in a new house – of course you bickered about how to furnish it.

Part of grieving is hating the changes it forces on

you. In order to adjust to your loss, you have to keep on letting your feelings go. So try to understand the rows.

Still weeping

My Mum died last year. I live with my aunt and uncle. The thing is I now like reading the death page in the newspaper. I don't know why, but also when I'm reading I start to cry. I'm busy enough, always in my bedroom doing homework or watching Neighbours, EastEnders *and other things, but maybe I still miss her? It's been nearly a year. From Dawn.*

'Course you still miss her. I hope you always feel it would have been better had she lived. Grieving for someone usually takes at least a couple of years and you often get sadder when the anniversary comes.

The death pages are being a sort of friend by giving you the chance to have a weep. Don't worry, you haven't turned into a vampire and you're not morbid!

Talk about your Mum to your aunt or uncle. Say you want to know what she was like as a child. See if they have any stories about what she got up to. The easier it becomes to mention her name I promise the better you will feel.

Wish to die?

I have a problem. The closest boy I have ever met has died and several times I have nearly killed myself but I know I wouldn't. I don't think I can survive without him. Please help. Mary, aged 11.

I don't believe you are going to kill yourself either.

I think your letter means: 'This was the nicest boy I ever knew. When he died, my heart broke. It felt like I would never enjoy myself again. I get sad all through. It's like the bit of me that can fall in love has been killed. I don't know how to bear these feelings.'

Grief does this to you. You will survive. But just for a while, you will feel as if your life has also stopped. Please tell someone how much it is hurting.

Dead dog   1

This April my dog Toting died and I keep crying. Toting came from the North Pole and was very rare. One day recently at school, I couldn't work. What shall I do?
Sad Lad.

Well, don't be ashamed of being sad. I'm sure you loved your dog so it would be surprising if you were *not* upset. Put your sorrow into words to take the pressure off. That's the reason why you've had trouble working. You need to tell someone all you feel about Toting.

Dead dog   2

My problem is that my dog has just died. Whenever I say she has had to be put down (it was cancer), I start to get upset. Devon Girl.

Of course you do. If something is inevitable, invite it. Make a special time to think about your pet. Get comfy, cuddle a hot-water bottle, look at photos of her and let your tears flow. Tell your family this is how you feel. If you do that once a week for a while, you'll stop getting ambushed by grief.

To the funeral?

A friend of mine has just died in a tragic drowning accident, one day after his 13th birthday. Me and my friends cannot believe it. We are totally devastated and I don't know how to control my feelings. There are so many things I want to say and do to help his parents. So far I have bought a sympathy card and I took it round the class for everyone to sign. But I also want to go to his funeral. Is this a good thing to do? Anon.

Sure, because funerals are designed to help those left behind learn how to cope with their loss. You feel the need to show you care. The service might also allow you to shed your tears and relieve some sorrow. What isn't so good is to 'control' your sadness, although I realise you are afraid of it. Don't worry, tragic news always has to sink in slowly and it's perfectly normal to be frightened by shock. Your heart is in the right place and your feet should take you to the service. You'll feel a lot better afterwards.

A laughing matter?

My friend and I have a big problem and we both feel awful. You see, we always seem to laugh at things that are really sad. For instance, one of our teachers told us that her father had died and we looked at each other and cracked up, giggling like mad (fortunately the teacher didn't see). We both feel guilty as anything about it. We don't understand and nobody else seems to understand why we're like this. Two Anxious Teenagers Still At School.

Try not to worry. It's very common to laugh when you are shocked or embarrassed. What you are saying is that sadness disturbs you almost too much. (Maybe you're unused to talking about 'difficult' things at home?) For whatever reason, you cannot handle these feelings, so in class the tension comes out through a safety valve of giggles. It would be helpful to spend more time chatting privately about the things that upset you. These may be famine in Africa, cruelty to animals, cancer, as well as people dying. Then when such issues crop up, you'll be readier to cope.

Losing Cynthia

It feels quite weird to write this but I have a friend called Cynthia and she is 10 years old. Funnily enough, it is a car! Some time soon we are going to have to sell her because we now have a new car and I just don't know what to do.

My Mum and Dad do not know anything about this letter. I am only eight and it has been hard even to post it. Mary, London.

When you think about it, Mary, your feelings make complete sense. Cynthia is a friend. You have given her a name. You grew up in her. She is a bit like a Mummy. You have known her *all* your life. She has looked after you. Cynthia is part of your memory. She has taken you to happy (and sad) events (going to parties; maybe going to casualty at hospital). And now you have to say goodbye to her.

I suggest you hold a special farewell ceremony when the time comes and take photos. If your parents don't understand, that's their problem, but you be true to what you feel. It will always help you in life to know how to let go.

Sad videos

I don't know where to start because I'm all mixed up. I was watching Cat Among The Pigeons *by Bros yesterday. There are parts of it where Matt Goss gets really hurt and confused and I wanted to stop that happening. I wanted to reach out and protect him and look after him. I was crying so much because I couldn't. I really care about him and I just wanted to stop him feeling so sad.*

I know it was only a video and he was only acting but I just couldn't stop my feelings. What should I do? I'm 14. Sally, Leeds.

Never be ashamed of what you feel. Plenty of adults go to a movie and bawl their eyes out. (Even though it's only a film put together by people trying to make a profit.) We all get moved by drama.

Your emotions are growing just like your body. You have new ways of feeling sympathy.

So don't be surprised when this happens. Get to know this developing side of yourself which seeks to care and protect. Maybe you can also see that it gives you a safe outlet for feelings about someone or something else?

When you were six you were probably into fun and presents. Now you've moved on. Today, you are much more likely to notice other people's moods of distress – even when it's a performance for camera.

Depression 1

Two weeks ago I was very ill and I have just got better. The problem is I have not been eating and a few days ago I ate nothing. My friends have said I still look very ill. When I try to eat, the food puts me off. Also I have been upset over small things. Everyone asks me what's wrong but I say nothing's wrong. It is all getting to me. I fear I want to kill myself as nothing goes right any more. NKOTB fan.

You are depressed for two reasons. First, not eating will make you gloomy anyway. Starving the brain of food makes you feel *rotten*. It's a purely physical reaction, so get chewing. Secondly, you are down because of illness and other worries. Your depression tells you life is all bad. Never talking keeps you stuck in this point of view. I guarantee this misery would lighten if you did start opening up to others. And you'd also get your appetite back once the stress was relieved.

Depression 2

This may sound a really stupid problem, but I feel living is a complete waste of time. I get worried about things easily and end up putting myself through hell. It's small things that add up and make me feel awful.

Don't get me wrong. My family are loving and caring, but I don't feel confident enough to talk to them. To me life is just living, then going through hell, then dying.

I know there are good times, but mine seem to be bad. Please help. Helen, aged 14.

First, your problem isn't stupid. You explain clearly that you are feeling shy, anxious and depressed. Anyone who felt that way would be under loads of stress.

Secondly, feelings are real even if they aren't always true. You feel life is hell. You may be wrong, but that's what your insides tell you.

Thirdly, you are cut off. You are scared to talk. Human beings aren't built to live alone. When they do get isolated, they become unhappy, like you. In this situation, your mind can play any miserable trick on you it likes.

Above all, you are stuck because you don't let yourself go. If you could just pick one friend, explain what you've told me, then let the tears flow, your body would say thanks and relax. Then there's be room for some happier times.

CHAPTER 6

Stop teasing me!

Latin tease

*Two years ago, I decided to learn Latin. I told my Mum
and Dad I didn't like it, but they wouldn't let me pack it
in. It wouldn't be so bad if it was spoken but it's dead
and as far as I am concerned I soon will be.*

*I've now been doing Latin for two years and I'm at a
new school. Everyone keeps calling me swot and a snob
but they don't realise how much I hate it. In fact I've
just thrown my Latin books out of the window. Please
help. Mark – a very depressed teenager.*

You don't like Latin much (and I hope you didn't
hit anybody with your books) but you have coped
with it for 96 weeks. You know what your parents
want. I don't think learning Latin is the real
trouble. I think you are anxious and depressed
about being teased.

Naturally, you'd like to be popular. Naturally,
you want to be part of the crowd. However, you
also have to be yourself. If not, you will disappear
as a nobody.

You've got a good brain, so let's use it. Solve
your problem in four stages by saying: '1 I can't
stop Latin. 2 I can't stop the Bash Street Kids from
calling me names at school. 3 In any case, they
only do it because they feel a little threatened. But
4 I can still laugh and joke with them, despite the
teasing, and this will show them I'm not a freak but
OK to know.'

Everyone hates me

*Please help. There are 40 people in my class and most of
them hate me. I've two friends but I don't really like
them. I know that most people hate me because every
month our class does a silly survey. They ask everyone*

(except me) to name four boys they hate and four girls. My name crops up nearly every time. I've tried to be what they want but every time I get thrown aside. Please print this because I often cry myself to sleep. Don't say talk to your parents because I have and they just say I'm silly. NKOTB lover.

I'd feel bad in your shoes, so tell your parents they haven't understood your problem. (You can show them this letter if you like.) They think you're saying the whole world hates you. This is clearly not true. You have friends. What you mean is: 'I get teased at school and feel unpopular. I get sad and angry and hurt and need some comfort. Will you please be nice to me?' If they could do this, you would even become more popular at school! Kids always pick on the ones who are attention-hungry and desperate to please.

Ganged up on

Please help me – my two best friends keep making fun of me. I try to ignore them but it upsets me and I can't do it back because two against one is impossible with their quick answers. H.A. aged eight and a bit.

When something is impossible, go with it. Say nothing. Let these friends take their bit of fun. The sooner they stop, the sooner you will recover. If they go on and on, they're not friends at all, and you will pack them in because people do 'make up and break up'.

New school blues

I am a 10-year-old girl (nearly) and I'm scared about going to secondary school. You see I'm a bit chubby plus

I've been told some stories about secondary schools. Is there anything you can do about it? Love Toni.

Yes, I can let you know that everyone feels anxious when they change schools. It's always a bit worrying to leave the place you know for one you don't. So you're not ill, just normal.

Then I can get you to prepare for problems. If you're going to get teased (and who doesn't?), then tell yourself they might just mention your size. So what's the worst thing they can say? Be prepared for it, so you don't get a shock or lose control. If you're ready for them, they can't win!

Next I can get you to ask your Mum or Dad to take you up to the school and look over it. Find out from a teacher or caretaker where your classroom will be and what the routine is. Then when Day One comes you will feel confident about what to do.

Soccer tease 1

I simpy hate PE. Everyone else in our class loves it. I can't play football and it bores me silly. Everyone says I am stupid and they call me names. I am 11 years of age. Please help. From a Kylie and Jason fan.

It would be a very silly world if we *all* liked and did the same things. You are also sensible in disliking games you cannot play. However, PE is necessary to keep you fit so you have to struggle through it. As for being teased about soccer, tell yourself: 'So what! We can't all have our brains in our feet.'

Soccer tease 2

I am not very good at football. Well, at least I think I

am not. My friends are always saying I am better than they thought. On Thursday, I am representing my House at football and I am worried that people will laugh at me. Even though I am in the 'C' Team, I don't want to let my house down. Have you any advice for me? A Bad Footballer.

Yes, you feel anxious and unconfident. This makes you ignore facts. Your friends know you can play. So does the House or they wouldn't have picked you.

Stop being a perfectionist. If you go onto the pitch saying 'I must never make a mistake', you'll probably screw up.

Tell yourself you can only try to do your best. Even the top players sometimes score an own goal. And if it's possible for Gary Lineker to have an off-day, why should you be different?

Just give yourself a chance.

Soccer tease   3

I have written before, but my letter didn't get printed. People think I'm a girl. They call me Mavis. In PE, people laugh at me because I can't play football and according to them it makes me even more of a girl. Also they say I have a face like a girl and I talk like one. I just can't stand it much longer. A Kylie and Jason fan.

Oh yes you can, because you're going to win this battle. The truth is, people can say *anything* they like and you can't stop them. Well, can you? Tell me how? Shoot the lot? So having agreed you can't prevent others from teasing you, how will you learn to live through it? Generally, you get called a girl *because* you hate it so much. They know it works. It's no fun being got at, but it *is* fun to tune out and watch them get exhausted trying to wind you up. So when the name-calling starts, tell yourself inside that you're a perfectly normal boy who quite naturally hates football and that's that. Keep saying to yourself: 'Millions of people hate football and many of them are men.' If you can accept that these 'people' are free to shoot their mouths off, they'll eventually realise how boring they are.

Sits with girl

Please will you help me? You see I am really sick of my classmates skitting me just because I sit next to a girl. Even though I don't fancy her, Rosemary is a good friend who I sit next to in Art and Maths. She is my only friend and the other lads are driving me away. I am really distressed and don't want to sit and be on my own. Please tell me what to do because my life isn't worth living without Rosemary. Peter, 14, Derbyshire.

Has it crossed your mind the lads might be envious? It's actually an achievement at 14 to have made a good friend with someone of the opposite sex. It shows you are quite grown up, and certainly mature enough to see this problem through.

The best response to teasing is smiling indifference. After all, the teaser only gets pay-off if you react, doesn't he? Carry on enjoying Rosemary's company in class and ignoring all the skits and the teaser is helpless.

The second-best response to teasing is to tease back. Grin and shout 'Jealous!' to the howling mob and you might enjoy needling them. But they can always stick it to you again. The best you can hope for is a shouting stalemate.

It does occur to me that if Rosemary's such a good friend she could give you some real support

– but only if you share the trouble. Tell her all about it, but not during lessons or the teacher might separate you anyway.

Boring boy

There is this boy at our school who keeps putting his arm round us and mouthing 'I love you' to us. It really is embarrassing because he does it in public. We are only 10 and it is very irritating. We have tried telling our parents but they just say to ignore him. How can you ignore such a thing as this? Badgered and Bothered.

Oh, you can. If he won't bug off, just have a discussion out loud about how much his breath smells. He'll shut up.

Stutter tease

Please help – every time I talk to anybody I always stutter and now it's just driving me crazy and all of my friends keep teasing me about it. Another thing is that I have hairs on my neck. Why is that? Depressed Person, Girl aged 12.

The best way to deal with a stutter is to make yourself speak much more slowly. Practise in private at first. This will help you avoid getting flustered. If the problem is severe, you can get help from the Stammerers' Association based in London (dial 142 to find out if they have a branch in your town). As for hair on the neck, we all have it. In fact, if you take a close look, you'll notice there are hairs everywhere on your body except on the palms of your hands and soles of your feet, some so fine you can only see them through a magnifying glass. I have to add that lots of people think neck hairs are very attractive!

Tantrum

*I have a very bad temper which I can't control. If my
brother starts to tease me, I get very cross and hurt him.
Please help me to calm myself down. Anon.*

Right, memorise his typical teases. When he trots
them out, simply say 'Boring'. Keep saying this till
he gets tired. This is better and safer than hitting
him. Then when you're alone, stand in front of a
big mirror and tell your reflection exactly what
you think of your yucky brud, just to let off steam.

Vege-tease

*I am a nine-year-old girl and have recently become
vegetarian. I've told a few of my friends at school but
they tease me. One of them said, 'What if you weren't on
packed lunches and there was meat on the menu?' I
think that if you're vegetarian, you're still a normal
person, but why do they keep teasing me? A Kylie and
Jason fan from Blackpool.*

They tease you because you want to be different
from them and it feels like criticism. So they attack
back. Their line about lunch is beside the point
since you *do* have sandwiches. Stick to your guns
and they'll get used to you. How many of them are
still eating beef, by the way?

Glasses tease

*I have a horrid problem. I was seven and I had to go to
the opticians and start wearing glasses part-time for
reading, writing and watching TV. I did this at home,
but never at school. Now the optician says I must wear
them full-time. I am also really unhappy at school*

because I am bullied. How can I avoid using glasses and being laughed at? Anon.

Your problem is not glasses – which are cool, fun and useful because they keep things like flies from getting in your eyes. Your problem is about being teased and bullied. You are terrified people at school will pick on your specs as a new way to have a go. First, see if you can have some specs that really are attractive. Second, tell yourself if someone does call you four-eyes it only proves they lack both originality *and* brains. Don't reply, just get on with what you are doing but tell your Mum at the end of the day that some people really are a big pain and can you have a moan.

   If you don't react, they will give up.

School tease

There is this girl in my class whom I hate. She is always saying horrid things about me. The thing is she SITS by me in school and I can't stand it any longer. At one time, my pen was squeaking so she pulled my hair and punched me. I've tried avoiding her and moving places but it doesn't work. Please help me. A Tiffany fan.

Moving places *will* stop her beating you up in lessons. But nothing can stop her saying nasty things about you since being grotty is *not* against the law. All you can do is bore her to death by yawning every time she teases. It's because you 'bite' that she bothers to go 'fishing'.

Cure for teasing

I am writing to you to give hope to anyone like me. I am not really fat but I'm not slim either. When people say things about me, I just laugh at them and say something about myself back and create a giggle. I am not self-conscious at all now. I used to be, but it's gone. I have made loads more friends out of boys and I just have a great time. And as long as I wear the right type of clothes, I can look great. Please try to print this because I would like to help people like me. Love, Rebecca Sellars.

Will do, because I think you are right. Many of us are built big and chances are we will stay that way. So the rest of the world better adapt!

CHAPTER 7

Trouble with my family and friends

Divorce pains

My mother and father are getting a divorce. My mother goes out sometimes and when she does my father gets angry. He starts saying it's my fault for them breaking up. He then gets out a belt and beats me and my brother. Can you send me some advice because I'm scared. My mother and father both hate me. I'm sorry my writing's shaky, but he's just hit me. Please help. Thank you. Anon.

It cannot be your fault that your parents are divorcing. If they fail to cope with their children that's down to them. You are probably being blamed because it's easier for them to do this than face up to their real problems.

Second, while smacking you may be accepted, assaulting you is a crime. If you haven't got a grandparent, aunt or uncle who can protect you and your brother, then choose a teacher at school whom you really trust (think hard about this) and tell them the whole story. If the beatings are serious (and tell the truth), that teacher can contact a local authority social worker and help take out a Place of Safety order, so you won't be abused any more.

Third, it may feel as though your parents both hate you but they are under great stress. Just suppose your Mum does not know what is happening when she's out? Again, it may be easier to get another member of the family to tell her.

But – please let me know how it goes on.

Can't talk to mum   1

At school I never have any good friends. I am not horrible, I don't tease or bully anyone or get bossy. When I was in hospital just before Christmas people from school sent get-well cards – but I know they don't really like me – ALSO I can't talk to my Mum or anyone else about sex and boys and when I should wear a bra. My Mum would probably be surprised and cross and say I should not know yet. But people at school are always talking about them. But I'd rather know about it from my Mum. Lisa.

You've got a bit cut off so now you're suspicious of everyone. However, we both know that nasty people don't get sent cheer-up cards. I suggest you are disturbed by the changes in your body and maybe your Mum has *not* been really aware of this. You have to give her a chance, put her in the picture. I don't suppose she's really such a rat-bag, especially if you open her eyes by saying you really need to discuss growing-up pains generally. Get a copy of my first book, *Growing Pains* (BBC Books), from the library to help. There are sections on friendships, as well as starting your periods.

Can't talk to mum   2

I am 14 and my problem is I can't talk to my Mum. I love her very much but we only talk about school and careers. I am not a shy person – in fact the opposite. I've been asked to go out by lots of boys but always say no because I can't discuss it with my Mum first and would get embarrassed. Last week, my friends asked if I wanted to go the New Kids On The Block concert. I said no because I couldn't pluck up the courage to ask my Mum and knew she'd say no, too. NKOTB fan.

Well, you're not shy, but you do seem easily embarrassed. I think this feeling must get in the way when it comes to talking about the things you want to do. So don't dismiss it.

You need to recognise that you won't go up to Mum and begin a major debate about sex and boyfriends tomorrow!

So, why not ask if you can have a bunch of friends around of both sexes one weekend afternoon? Work out what you're going to say in advance. Practise out loud. Think of all your Mum's likely reactions. Choose the best time to pop the question (when she's neither tired nor hungry). Imagine her saying a big loud 'yes' to give you confidence.

You could also begin having more personal conversations with her by asking some questions about life when she was 14. Most people do like to talk – about themselves!

Too caring dad

I have got a problem with my Dad. He is over-protective. I get so angry with him. Sometimes, I even cry because I am so angry. I feel like running away but I don't think I will. He cares so much about me. He wants me to go to the school he's chosen whereas I want to go to school with my friends. Unhappy VC.

You have to see that your Dad has power on his side. He loves you. He is responsible for you but also controls you. Therefore, it is difficult to influence him. Sit him down. Say you understand why he wants the best for you. But explain that you are going to be miserable losing your friends. Tell him you are upset anyway about going to a new school. And show him you are growing up by sounding like an adult. You may not get the school you want, but you will start to open his eyes.

Stepdad blues

I have a stepdad that is always telling me off for very little things. Like if I leave a few things out in my bedroom he really shouts at me. I have only got one friend who understands this problem. My Mum doesn't know what happens to me. He doesn't let me watch programmes that I like – programmes like Neighbours *and* Round the Twist, *and I don't see why he sees so much harm in them – and he tells me off for saying that I should be allowed to see them. What shall I do? From a Very Unhappy Reader.*

Start by telling your Mum in clear and simple words what the problem is. Ask if she can help you deal with these things? Explain that you understand your stepdad needs to get used to you. His standards are different (and he has a blindspot about *Neighbours*!). But if you promise to clear up your room as he wants, will he let you see your favourite serial? This is a fair offer.

Horrible sister

Every time I get angry with my sister, I end up slapping her, then I feel better. But I always get told off and she mostly gets her way. I've tried everything. Please, please, please can you help me? Les, Bristol.

Well, you haven't tried everything. All you do is repeat yourself and get into trouble. That's not clever, is it? I know teasing hurts. But of course your parents won't let you bash people who do it, especially your sister.

Try *not* hitting her. Then she won't get instant sympathy from your Mum and Dad. And she'll lose her power over you.

Avoid using your fists by listing all the names she calls you then ticking them off in your head as she feebly attempts to wind you up. Grin every time she falls into this trap. And enjoy this new feeling of control.

Mad dad

Please help me. I am 11 years old and have two sisters, one seven and one 10 months. We visited my nan's and phoned home at 10.00 to say we would be late. We got home at 10.30. We were sent straight to bed. Our Dad was really mad because it was pub closing time. Before we got home, he rang my nan and took it out on her. My Mum grabbed my Dad and almost burst his kidney with the car key. He is covered in bruises. On Monday he apologised to our nan. I love them both very much. Please help. I'm scared. A NKOTB fan.

I think I'd feel frightened if my parents were having such violent rows. Please tell yourself very, very seriously that *none of this is your fault.*

When the adults don't cope, your job isn't to take the blame but to say: *'Stop it, you're scaring me.'*

Tune out as much as you can, but when the noise is too much tell them how upset you feel.

Hot spot for pop

I know this sounds funny, but I have a hot spot for my Dad and I am too shy to tell him. But I think he knows. It pleases him. Naomi, aged 10.

I'm sure your Dad is aware that you admire him.

That's great, and normal. You don't need to spell it out, but if you want to say something, just tell him . . . he's great!
(PS – you can't marry him. He's spoken for.)

Divorce sadness

Please help – when I see something sad on TV, I get very emotional and I can't control it, even if it's only a cartoon. I also start to cry when people shout at me. It's embarrassing because I can't stop crying. I also get sad because my Mum and Dad are divorced but that was when I was a baby. I am 10 now, 11 in April. I also get emotional when I try to talk to people about personal stuff. A depressed FF fan.

I can see that you are very unhappy about the divorce *now* because you would like two parents to share your problems with at home, but you don't have them. It's grief leaking through again, reminding you what's gone wrong in your life.

You have never accepted these sad feelings, which is why they ambush you. Please talk to whichever parent you feel closest to. Don't apologise for sounding depressed. Explain why you feel unhappy and ask them to let you talk without arguing or advising, just give you a hug.

Wants more from mum

I have a problem. Sometimes I cry myself to sleep. It never gets any better. It's my Mum. I know she loves me, but she never seems to show it. She has lots of children and I'm just one of them. They are all my half-brothers and sisters and she treats them really nice. She always agrees with them and gives them anything. I've tried to get close, but she ignores me. My Dad is always at work so I feel lonely. At school, I'm very outrageous and have got into lots of trouble because of wanting attention. I do this because I don't get it at home. My school has a counsellor, but I don't feel my problem is serious enough to go to her. I want to hurt myself so they will notice. I've also considered suicide. Distressed 16-year-old.

I'm sure your Mum doesn't really know how terrible you feel. I'm also sure she may find her other children easier to deal with and therefore seems to favour them. But this is only because you are at a very needy stage in your life – a 'handful' as they say.

However, this does not mean you have no problems, does it? You feel so bad about yourself you don't even feel entitled to use the school counsellor!

Ask yourself this: if a school counsellor isn't willing to talk to a girl who feels suicidal, just what is she for? Please go and make an appointment.

Mum into meat

I'm 10½ and I hate the idea of killing animals just for the sake of humans eating. It's like a cow saying I'm hungry, I'll go and kill a human! I'm not a vegetarian, but I've thought about it and I want to be one. My problem is that I have tried to tell my Mum, but she keeps on giving me meat to eat. Please help, a Fast Forward *Megafan.*
PS – Do vegetarians eat cheese?

You're entitled to your view, although most people would say cows are not so important (or as clever) as people. Hindus, however, who nearly worship cows, would say that you are right. And, anyway, you're entitled to become vegetarian if you wish.

However, you must recognise that this will cause your parents extra work with the shopping and cooking. So ask them nicely and offer to help. In the last resort, if you refuse to eat meat, they won't force-feed you.

As for cheese, many vegetarians eat it because no animal is killed to make cheese. In fact, cows would get jolly uncomfortable if the raw material (milk) wasn't emptied out of them!

Is she adopted?

We think our friend is adopted, because she is nothing like her parents or relatives in build or personality. Her Mum is too young to have had her. It wouldn't matter to us if she were adopted, but we'd like to know because lately she has been really moody and upset. Is there any way we could find out if she was adopted? And should she be told by a certain age? She's 13 now. Please help, from two New Kids' fans.

First, you can't tell if someone's adopted by looking. Tall parents with dark brown skins could have short children with light brown skins. Second, medical problems in pregnancy and illness afterwards can affect the size, weight and shape of any child. Third, you must remember that a young-looking Mum could be as much as ten years older than you think. Fourth, a woman can get pregnant from her early teens onwards. Fifth, everyone gets moody and upset from time to time. Sixth, adoption is a *confidential* process. The only person with a 'right to know' is the adopted child when grown up. So last (and here's the crunch) this is not your business so please don't go making a tough situation worse. I know you care, but being a friend means *not* solving other people's problems unless invited.

Rows with big brother

I am writing to tell you about my brother Mike. Seven years ago, my little brother Alan was born and since then my big brother Mike has started rows about everything. Long before my small brother Alan was born, Mike and I used to play together. Now he won't even look at me. If I try to talk, he won't listen. If my finger as much as brushes his dinner plate, he can't eat a thing. I wish my baby brother wasn't born, but what can I do? Bothered Boy.

I guess Mike is angry because he has to share with you and Alan. If there are three of you, he perhaps now gets one-third of the attention whereas before he could have it all. I don't think you will help matters by retaliating. Your best bet is to tell your Mum and Dad you worry about Mike. Could they assist by making more time for him and getting closer to him? He clearly needs it.

No appetite for divorce

My problem is that my parents are getting divorced and I'm not eating. I'm getting thinner and thinner. Once my Mum nearly had to force me. I'd dread to think what will happen when they get divorced. I can't eat even if I try. I do not show my problems at school but inside I need help. Please advise me and be QUICK! Anon.

You cannot eat because you are full of fear. Fear of

the future, fear of losing touch with your Dad (or Mum), fear of moving away from your present home.

You probably have lots of nervous acid in your stomach because of this anxiety. You may even feel perpetually sick.

I'm sorry you feel so terrified of talking about your problems because doing this would help you *most*. Anxiety always gets relieved if you can cut it down to size by putting it into words. It's the best method of controlling your imagination.

Try to talk to a teacher, relative or friend. At the very least, ask your parents to give you some news of their plans. You're entitled to ask because it all affects you too.

When you've done this, you will stop alarming your stomach and be able to feel normal hunger again.

Rows at home

I have a problem. Recently, I have had a lot of worries about arguing at home. And it's affecting me at school. If a teacher gets angry with anyone and starts to shout, I cry because there is so much shouting at home.

A teacher has asked me what's wrong, but I am too embarrassed to say. I am shy and find it difficult to communicate with people.

I have a teacher whom I think I can trust. Should I tell her about my problems? If I did tell her, what could she do? Unhappy Boy, aged 12.

Yes, please tell her your problems when you can. Just putting it into words is going to help. It will take some of the scary pressure off you.

Perhaps you will gain enough confidence to take further, practical steps – such as telling your parents that home is hard. But only when you're ready to say this, of course.

Finally, don't put yourself down. Your letter is clear and well-written so it is not true that you cannot communicate with people, although I realise you feel anxious about doing so at the moment.

More rows

The problem is my Mum and stepdad. They are wonderful and give me and my sister everything but they are always rowing about money. My stepdad works long shifts up to 12 hours with overtime.

They had a big argument which they thought I couldn't hear about him wanting to go to the pub to give someone some money when my Mum thought they could sit and spend some time together. The shouting got louder till they said it wasn't worth staying together. My Mum said she would split us up. I might have to go and live with my real Dad with my sister staying here.

Could they split us up? Is it the law? Please write back at once cos all I'm doing is crying. My other friends don't have families that argue like this. Anon.

Which shows you that all families are different. And listening to rows is often more upsetting than taking part in them. Haven't you ever shouted 'I hate you!' to a friend? Did you really mean it, *forever*?

Tell your Mum how anxious you are about the future. Say you couldn't help hearing her threaten to walk out. Explain you are grateful for all their hard work. But can you have some reassurance about where you are going to live?

If it's true, let her know you don't want to go back to your Dad. Alas, you cannot choose where to live – they are in charge. But it would be fair to ask for lots of time to get used to any changes. So could she give you early news?

Rows again

My Mum is going through a rough time at the moment and she's blaming it on my Dad. She is saying some awful things like he never does anything for her. They have been rowing for as long as I can remember. Please help me. Unhappy Boy, 10.

Children have needs, whatever their parents are suffering. You need to be able to ask your Mum to give you a break. Sure, she has problems. But it won't help her to make your life just as miserable.

Ask her to talk about your Dad to other people (grown-ups, marriage counsellors) but *not to you.* In fact, tell her you are not prepared to listen because you can't divorce your Dad even if she can. Kids need to stay friends with *both* parents while she is tearing you in two.

Tough dad

I hate my Dad. When he gets home from work, he's always in a bad mood. He starts shouting and smacking me. Sometimes I deserve it, but most of the time it's my sister's fault. She's younger than me and really annoying. She teases me and gets me so mad. Please print this letter as I have no one to talk to. A Waterfront *fan. Cornwall.*

It's reasonable to hate your Dad's behaviour, but it's not clever to let your sister keep getting you into trouble. I guess she winds you up to the point where you use your strength to bash her. She tells your parents. Then your Dad bashes you.

Face facts. Your sister is a tease. You can't stop her. Your Dad is tired when he comes in. You can't stop him. You don't like getting punished. You can avoid it. Just let your sister tease you without hitting back.

Try it for two days. See what it's like *not* to get into trouble with Dad.

Pesky brother

Just now my brother has been playing with the boy from across the road. I understand that my brother has to play with somebody, but I don't feel safe in my own home. When I get changed they go into my bedroom and when I am playing records they come jumping in. Please help – my brother is not usually naughty. I think I will not survive if something isn't done. Love, Suzie, aged 9, Manchester.

I know what you mean – you feel so invaded, you don't know where to put yourself. It's as if your head will explode.

Even so, I *know* you are going to survive, and so do you, really.

Your bruddy is showing off pushing you around. You've got to stand up for yourself.

I think you're old enough to ask your Dad to fit a small bolt to the inside of your bedroom door so that you can be private there. Tell him you only want a titchy one so that in any emergency he could break it open.

Then if your brother comes along, he can only enter by force and risking a big row.

Guilt trip from mum

I'm a girl of 15 living with my mother because my

parents are separated. They always used to argue, but now my mother takes it out on me when things go wrong. Since my little sister was born, my Mum has lost contact with all her friends and she doesn't go out any more. So each time I want to go somewhere with friends, I don't dare to ask her because she'll say something like 'You go and enjoy yourself, don't mind me!' Ironically meant though. And then I feel guilty. I have become totally isolated and have few friends left. If I try to talk to her about it, we always end up arguing. I'm afraid it will affect my future. Anon.

I agree – I also think it will affect your Mum's future. You both need your feelings to move on – you must see your friends and have a social life – it's both a need and a right. This means not letting yourself get manipulated by Mum's guilt-making comments. She needs to realise she cannot *'marry'* you – you cannot be her replacement partner. So both problems – yours and hers – are helped if you can learn to say: 'Yes, I see you don't like being alone, but I need to go out with my friends tonight – tara.' Offer her a deal in return. Say you'll baby-sit any Wesnesday or Friday night when she's feeling ready to go out. If you do spend all your free evenings at home, your Mum can stay depressed for ever – but at your expense.

Father mystery

I live with my mother and stepfather. I like him very much. But my real father died before I was born. Could you tell me how I could ask my mother more about him? And what kind of person he was? Without upsetting my stepfather? Donna, 12, Wales.

Your letter is wise and thoughtful, so I am sure you will handle this well.

All you have to say to your Mum is what you mean: 'I don't want to upset stepdad. I don't want to make you sad. But I really need to know something about my other father. It would help me if you could tell me a bit about him. Will you? I think I'm old enough now.'

Perhaps show your Mum this letter. Everyone needs to know where they come from, don't they? And this 'stranger' is part of you, isn't he?

Choosing your parent

I'm 11 years old. My parents are about to be divorced and I have to choose who I want to live with and I want to live with my father, but I just don't know how to tell my mother.

I really love her, but I prefer to live with my father. I would stay with my mother every weekend, but during the week I would live in Manchester with my Dad, where I have lots of family and get on with them really well. Please tell me how to tell my Mum. Anon.

You're in a no-win position – which you've been put in. The way to tell your Mum is to say: 'Well, what I really want is for the break-up not to happen – but obviously I cannot have what *I* want. So I've got to compromise. The answer is that I'd rather be in Manchester with my family and friends and see you at weekends.' Reassure your poor old Mum that you love her (say it), but alas you cannot split yourself in two as well.

Rifles mum's things

I want to tell you my secret, but I am very ashamed of it and I don't feel those around me care enough about me to listen. My problem is too complicated to go into, but my secret is that when my Mum is away I look through all her drawers and read her letters. I know that this is an awful thing to do and if she found out she would be really angry and upset, but I can't help it. Once I tried to tell her that all I wanted was for her to love me and look after me and I said that I wanted support. She laughed. I'm falling behind with my school work and I've got mocks coming up soon. I'm 16. Please help. Anon.

First, rifling is not all that uncommon a thing to do – the usual motive is curiosity because your parents have had a long life before you were born. However, your motive is more – I feel you're trying to get closer to your Mum by discovering her intimate secrets. This is sad – it means you feel quite cut off from her to start with. But don't despair or give up. Instead of asking Mum to love you more – something she cannot quite deal with – ask her to tell you what she was like at 16. She'd probably enjoy that – and it's a way of getting her to open up to you. The relationship between you is poor, so you have to build things gradually. (And good luck with the exams.)

Sisters!

My problem is my sister. When she takes my things from my room, I go and get them back. Then she starts scratching and hurting me. Then my Mum comes in and sees me holding her. And this is the worst part. My sister suddenly hesitates and starts pretending to cry. Then my

Mum blames me. I ask my Mum to believe me, but she just believes my sister. I always think 'It's Not Fair!!!' I hate my sister when she does what I call her 'act', so please give me some advice. From a frustrated 11-year-old.

You can't solve this problem in heat. You must tackle your parents when your sister is *not* being a menace. First, ask if you can have a box or chest which is lockable. Then put your most precious possessions into it. (You could even make this a birthday or Christmas request.) Second, explain to your parents that your sister does cry sometimes to get her way, so could they please bear this in mind next time there's a dispute? Third, don't keep repeating your mistakes. If your sister takes something you need, explain the problem to a grown-up and ask what you are supposed to do about it? You could also say to yourself: do I really need it back this minute? If you stopped responding, your sister might stop provoking you.

Prisoner at 12

I have a problem which not many people have. I'm not allowed out. I'm not even allowed to go down town on my own. I have asked my friend what to do and she said that I should talk to my Mum and ask her why I'm not allowed out. I have asked my Mum before, but she wouldn't say anything. She wouldn't answer. I'm nearly 12 and I need your help. From H.

Learn not to give up just because you don't succeed first time. Ask your Mum to talk to you again. If she won't, say when can you talk to her? When she talks, say when can you start going out a bit? If she says, 'Not yet,' ask her does she mean not three months, half a year, next year, not for five years – what does she mean? This will help you negotiate and reach an acceptable compromise (since you're not going to get everything you want, are you?)

Drunken fights

I am 11 years old and my Mum fights all the time with her boyfriend called Tony. They shout and slam doors and it scares me a lot. I've tried talking to them about it, but they just blame each other. It is mainly through drink. My Mum says that she will get rid of him, but she just hasn't got the heart. I am very scared. Please help me. Very worried, from Milton Keynes.

I think you are in a rotten fix and doing very well just to get by. Anyone would be scared by this, so give yourself a big gold star for coping.

Then tell yourself you also need extra help. There are special organisations which can assist, such as AL-ANON and AL-ATEEN. They give support to anyone who is forced to live with a problem drinker. This means you. Find out about them by ringing the Milton Keynes Alcohol Advisory Service. The number is 668603. Use a coin box if you prefer. If you are outside Milton Keynes, ring AL-ANON on 01-403 0888 (10 am–4 pm, weekdays).

Brotherly love

I have two problems. There is a boy who lives in my street and goes to the same school. He pinches my bottom and says 'Hi, Doll!' every day. I have tried taking different routes to school but he just follows me. My second problem is I love my brother to pieces (he is 14 and I'm 12) and one day we kissed. Have we done wrong? Anon.

It sounds to me as though you don't talk enough to other people. Stop avoiding this boy. (Tell him to take a long walk off a short pier or your parents (or the police) will be round to sort him out.) As long as you keep running away, he'll go on doing it.

Secondly, it is nice that you like your brother, but he can't be your boyfriend and you need to discuss with your parents trying to improve your social life, going out more, having parties etc. PS – It's not wrong to kiss your brother, but the law says you cannot marry him.

Pet hate

I badly want a pet. My Mum agrees, so does my sister, but my Dad hates pets (I want a mouse). I have tried nagging, asking and everything I can think of. He is always cross and every time I ask he yells at me. Please help me. A Desperate Jason Donovan fan.

Maybe you *can't* have what you want, but let's give it one big try.

First, nagging is a lousy way to influence people. Saying things twice never strengthens your argument. You probably make things worse not better.

Second, if your Dad is under pressure, choose your moment to speak carefully *when he's most relaxed.*

Third, don't plunge in. Ask him when he will be able to spare you half an hour to talk something through? He might make you wait, but that's OK.

Fourth, anticipate his objections. If he hates

mess, say you'll keep your pet outside. If he's really difficult, say you'll keep your pet at a neighbour's house (if this can be managed). At the very least, try to get him to agree to come to the pet shop and take a look at a mouse. Who knows, maybe he's been afraid of them for years and needs to learn how harmless they are?

PS – As a joke, say you could have asked for a Rottweiler, so isn't he lucky?

Problem sister

I have a problem with my younger sister of 15 who has been stealing money from our mother's purse. When I confronted her about this, she said she needed it to buy a record and promised to stop. The trouble is she hasn't stopped but now steals regularly from Mum and Dad, Grandad and also from me. I calculate she must be taking about £15 a week. I don't know what she needs it for because she isn't buying any records or make-up. Also when I asked her friend with whom she is supposed to be passing all her time what was going on, her friend said she hadn't seen her in months. My big fear is she may be taking drugs. My parents have noticed that her personality seems to have changed and asked me to keep an eye on her, but I just don't know what to do. Jane.

Either your sister is trying to buy friends, or drugs, or she's gambling, or being blackmailed. However, you are not her mother and I think it's a bit unfair that this problem has been dumped on you. I'd quite understand if you told your parents you are very worried about her, so could they please get on with the job of looking out for her? At the very least, they should be close enough to their own child to know roughly where she goes, who her friends are and what she's feeling. If they won't do their job, why not say to your sister: 'It's not my business, but I'm really scared for you – if you ever need help, just ask me.' And be ready to tell her the name of a local drugs' counselling service in your area – you can find this out from your Citizens' Advice Bureau or local library service.

Make new friends

Me and my friend have just made up after a big argument which lasted for a year. In that year we both made another best friend, but now we have a problem.

Our problem is that we have decided we would like to be best friends again, but we do not want to hurt our other friends. Please help two Home and Away *fans.*

Well, it's impossible to please everyone and still make choices. *You* tell *me* how it can be done.

If you really are going to be best buddies again, it cannot be kept a secret. The only reasonable thing to do is explain to all concerned before they find out for themselves.

Break the news gently and make sure you don't drop these people from your lives – after all, there could always be another *big argument*, couldn't there?

Falling out

I was very good friends with two girls called Louise and Kerry. When we went on a school trip to Marchant's Hill we had a fight and since last October we have not been friends. All my other friends have turned against me and I am very worried. I have tried to ignore them, but it's no use. Laura, London.

Ignoring your problems is like putting them in the

freezer, Laura. It just keeps trouble fresh.

We all get chilly towards those who fight with us, but in the end you have to thaw.

Try to show your old friends a new face. You could even apologise, if you think it would help. At the very least, showing that you can change and adapt will give them the chance to do the same.

At present, you are still sending them the message that you don't need them, when the truth is that you do.

Hurts her friend

Please help – my best friend is always going off me, and it's all my fault because I keep mucking around. The other day she said that her Mum had banned me from her house and I thought her Mum really liked me. I really want to be sensible and nice like my friend, but it's in my nature to be silly. I am always making fun of her because I am good at gymnastics and she is less so. Please print this letter – I know it sounds like a daft problem, but at the rate I'm going I won't have any friends left. A depressed gymnast, Cardiff.

I suggest you show your *friend* this letter. Deep down you like her, you are sorry for what you've done and you don't know how to make things right. She will feel nice about you for trying to sort it out.

The most obvious problem concerns the way you make her feel like a fat slug at gym. Why do you do this? Answer: because you feel generally insecure unless you can crow about your own athletic skills.

The truth is that hot shots never need to boast; they *know* they're good. You want to work out what your real anxiety is about, instead of putting down your friend.

This will help you tackle the actual problem. (Is it your parents? Is it schoolwork?) Then you might have a social life in the 1990s.

Rich friend

My Mum is going through a rough patch this year with money and all she can afford is the food we eat during the week. I have recently told my best friend who was pretty understanding till two weeks ago when she started to make me jealous on purpose.

On Saturday, we went up the town centre to get a cheap pair of jogging trousers for £2.99. I used two weeks' pocket money to scrape together £3 for the trousers and a pound for bus fare and something to eat. When we were there, I asked my best friend how much money she had and she took great pleasure in telling me she'd got £41.50. Same thing happened the next week – she boasted she had £32. Now she's planning to spend £25 on trainers and she's going to buy some £21 fashionable shoes and £20 dungarees.

Every week I get more jealous. I can't tell my Mum because she'll get upset and begin to cry. I can't understand why my friend wants to make me feel so jealous. Please help because I will soon lose my cool and my friend at the same time. X, aged 13.

It crosses my mind you may have other family problems you haven't mentioned. Perhaps Dad's away? Or gone? Could be that some of your desperation is about feeling deprived of people as well as hard cash.

Even so, it feels bad enough to be excluded from the financial goodies. At a time when you want to be like your friends, and style matters, you feel unable to buy the necessary.

However, you are also treating your friendship with this girl as if it couldn't survive a bit of criticism.

What's the relationship worth when you can't tell your friend she is being insensitive, even if you are feeling over-sensitive?

Say you know it isn't her fault that she has money when you don't, but make it clear that you *are* feeling touchy so could she keep her bank statements to herself – if only for your sake?

(Why does she do it? Well, secretly we'd all like to have a hold over our friends. But you sort her out.)

Penpals

How can I get a penfriend? Anon.

Send a stamped, self-addressed envelope to IFL Penfriend Service, PO Box 117, Leicester, LE3 6EE. Include a brief note giving your age and interests and they'll find you a penfriend in England, Scotland, Wales or Ireland. The service is free.

CHAPTER 8

Doing schoolwork

Better reader

*Please can you help me? I am not that good at reading
or spelling words. Once a week, I have to go out of a
lesson to read for 10 minutes. I am really worried about
it. How can I learn to read really well without any fuss?
Will not reading well affect my future? From a worried*
Home and Away *fan.*

Anyone who can read had to learn how to do it,
since reading is a skill. If you want to be any good
at it, you must practise (just as if you want to be
good at football you must practise).

So the crunch issue is how much of *your* time are
you prepared to give to reading in the evenings at
home? Would it be as much time as you give to
watching *Home and Away?*

How you read is important too. Don't rush;
don't skip; look up words you don't know and
write them down in a notebook. Learn them afterwards. Then your spelling will automatically
improve.

Always read books that you like. Ask the libra-
rian or a teacher to help you choose.

If you do this, sticking to the task, your reading
will steadily improve. So too will your chances of
one day getting a decent job. Or filling in forms to
get money. Hey – some people even read books
for fun!

Better writer

*I am 10 years old. My teacher tells me I write very
neatly . . . BUT our headmaster says I am very scruffy.
Please can you help me? What do you think of my
handwriting? From a very worried boy of 10½.*

For those who can't see it because we've printed your letter, let me say your handwriting looks neat, well-formed, nicely joined up, properly punctuated and a joy to read. However, I'm sure you took trouble over this. Maybe your head-master's point is that sometimes you're *not* quite so careful? Whatever was said, don't worry – your teacher will know you *best*.

How to study

I'm 11 years old and in my last year of middle school. We have lots of work, much of which is homework. The problem is I'm finding it difficult to do. I get home at 4 pm and say to myself, 'Right, I'm going to have a cuppa, and then get straight on with my work,' but I don't. I don't find the actual work difficult – it's just getting started. I turn on the TV and watch a programme and before I know where I am, it is nine o'clock. I have tried working in silence, but I can't. It gives me the excuse to stare into space. How can I start work? I don't want to get into trouble. I hope you can give me some advice. Neil. Bradford.

Don't switch on the TV. It's impossible to concentrate on bookwork *and* watch telly. If you can't stand silence, play some quiet music (forget the heavy metal).

Your problem is starting. If you could avoid the distractions of tea and TV, you could probably get stuck in. Most people have occasional problems with starting. Authors call it 'writers' block'. They make 15 phone calls and drink pints of coffee *instead* of typing 'CHAPTER ONE'.

Clever people learn to use rewards. Tell yourself you will earn a teabreak for five minutes *after* half an hour's work. Remind yourself you can watch

TV or a video *when* the homework is finished. Looking forward to treats like this is the best spur.

Stick to a routine and you'll make it a habit. PS – you can get a booklet on how to study called *Help* from Carodan Enterprises, First Drift, Wothorpe, Stamford, Lincs PE9 3JL. It costs (tell your parents) £2.25, including postage.

Career or love?

I am 16 and officially have 10 weeks left at school. Recently, I have been offered a position on a training course when I leave. I could also study a similar course at college. I really want to do well in life and feel this could be my best chance. As you know, pay is not much at first, but I am guaranteed employment and a good salary on completion of training. The problem is that I don't feel ready to leave school and close friends behind, especially the one I love who is younger than myself and will still be at school. I could always stay on at school and take A-levels, which would solve the problem, but may mean missing out on the training course and guaranteed employment. Please advise – Ben.

Careers matter, but so do personal feelings. It is always difficult in life to 'move on', but maybe you really aren't ready to lose these important friendships yet.

I suggest decent training will still be available to you at 18. You are obviously a boy of ability. However, if you start A-levels next year, you must take them seriously. It would be a mistake to waste time for a rubbish result.

My other thought is that it's not sensible to take life *too* seriously before you must. The proper purpose of teenage is to experiment. Plenty of time later on to play safe!

Drama scholar

My problem is about school. Ever since I was eight years old, I have wanted to go to a stage school but my Mum says I have to get a proper education. I know she is right, though I don't think I can stand it much longer. I am always getting low marks in my exams and many nights I stay up till about eleven o'clock doing homework. Next morning, I cannot concentrate because I'm so tired. I am good at acting and drama, also swimming, yet because of homework I don't get much of a chance to act in plays so probably will never excel in them. A depressed 11-year-old.

You have two problems. First, how to get trained in drama. Second, how to organise your school-work. I suggest you think about them separately.

Tell your parents you are ambitious to act. Remind them that stage schools also teach normal subjects. If they cannot get you a place, will they help you find acting lessons somewhere? Can you also join the local amateur dramatic group?

As for schoolwork, re-organise your time. It's silly to be tired in the mornings, so *always* go to bed early enough to sleep properly, even if the work isn't quite finished. Then, start homework one hour earlier than at present.

If you do this well, you might even star in the next school play.

More homework

My parents and I usually row about twice a day – usually about things I have not done, such as my piano and flute practice and homework. Sometimes I am frightened to say I've got homework because they nag me to do it. Because of all this rowing, my parents have

stopped my pocket money. Ignoring them hasn't helped.
Since I am an only child, the only people, or in my case
cat, I can talk to without being talked back to is Pepper
my moggy, but he does not take much interest in the
subject! I am nearly 11. Russell.

Both sides in your family seem stuck in a rut. They
nag, which is boring. You provoke them, which is
boring.

Question: is there or is there not going to be
homework? Yes? OK, accept it and negotiate when
you agree you will do it, *so long as* they agree not to
bang on about it. Offer this as a deal.

Question: do you really want or need to learn
both flute and piano? Both these instruments are
very difficult to master. Would you prefer to
choose one or the other? Are you learning these
instruments for yourself, or for them? See if you
can do another deal – one less instrument, less
practice overall, but better practice say on the
flute, if that's what you decide. (I know Pepper
would also be happier if you made less noise!)

Tough teach   1

We have a problem at school. Our teacher always seems
to pick on us. She is a pain. And when we do get into
trouble, she never gives us our say. Why do all the others
get away with it and we don't? Two depressed Oz Prog
fans.

Well, life isn't fair, is it? Some teachers are bril-
liant; some should go and look after criminals on
desert islands. Deal with her *as she is*, not how
you'd like her to be.

You also need to ask yourself whether there's
any connection between the way you behave and

how she treats you? Do you wind her up? Just a bit? Perhaps in *her* lessons you have to be extra careful. She is not going to change unless you do.

Think of her as like a really difficult pet dog, always biting and snarling. You keep your hands in your pockets then, don't you?

Tough teach 2

The problem is two of my teachers, Mr A and Mr B, keep picking on me for no reason at all. I try to be nice to them, but they will not accept it. The other day I got told off for talking to my mate. What should I do? Madonna fan.

The cheap answer is *not* to talk to your mate during lessons because you can see it annoys the teachers. They may not want you to be 'nice'. Just obedient.

But don't despair. Work out from what is said how they *would* like you to act, and do it. After a bit, they will switch their attention to someone else.

CHAPTER 9

Fears and attacks

Attacked at work

*I am a boy and am working on a market in Manchester.
My boss has a friend. I'll call him Mr X. Today he
caught me alone and made a 'pass' at me (so to speak).*

*I have not told my Mum anything, or anyone in fact.
I am very scared he may do it again. I need some
advice. Please help! I am only 13 years old. Anon.*

I'm sure you feel alarmed, but the last thing you
need to do is keep quiet about this. If you can't tell
your parents, could you tell some other adult –
teacher, uncle, older brother? You can also ring
Childline free – 0800 1111.

You may even be wrong about your boss.
Instead of giving you the sack, he may feel his
friend is totally out of order.

However, you also need to know how to behave
if the offence is repeated. This must be rehearsed,
so go into your room, look in the mirror, imagine
the man standing in front of you, stare him in the
eye, and practise saying: 'Don't ever do that to me
again. I'm not like that.' If you're sure he won't hit
you, it would be helpful to add, 'Or I'll tell!' And if
he doesn't get the message at once, say, 'Bug off,
elephant ears!'

Finally, avoid ever being alone with this man.

Dangerous Dad

*Please help me! I'm a 15-year-old very devoted Bros
fan. Ever since I was small, I've been beaten. Now that
I'm getting older, I'm becoming more frightened.*

*I live in a family of six. I'm the oldest. If any of my
brothers/sisters start crying for any reason, or do the
slightest thing wrong like knock over a drink, my Dad
hits me with anything in sight.*

Recently, I've been getting brushes/ends of sweeping brooms thrown at me direct to my head. All I can keep thinking of is I'm going to get a blood clot.

I lead a very miserable life. I cry myself to sleep at nights.

The reason I haven't been to see anyone about it is because I'm real scared.

Sometimes, he's OK. But other times he isn't. I keep saying to myself, 'Make the most of today.'

He also hits my brothers and sisters, but not like he hits me.

Please help me, I'm so frightened – Bros are the only people who keep me going. Worried Boy.

I was worried to get your letter and think you are right to feel scared. The problem comes down to this: if you don't tell, the beatings will probably go on or get worse. From the sound of your letter, you feel ready to talk, but it is still a big step. You could speak to a teacher or to Childline – 0800 1111. But I think you might prefer to contact your local branch of the Samaritans (in the phone book), because they have a lot of walk-in centres where you can see someone face-to-face *and they will treat what you say in confidence, telling no one else.* This would get you used to the idea of making a big change in your family life and help you see the options and work out a solution. I think action will have to be taken because even if you yourself manage to escape, your brothers and sisters will end up in the firing-line. What your father is doing is wrong as well as illegal.

Abused – uncle

My Mum is foreign so we go to visit my Nana, but I

have a problem over there. My uncle is deaf and a bit handicapped. When I arrive, I go to see his model dolls and he follows me. While my Mum is in the kitchen and my brother is in the garden, he locks the door then starts to abuse me. I can't tell my Mum because it would hurt her feelings. I have talked about it to my friend at school, and her sister.

While I am at school, I cry and get upset. My three other friends asked me what was wrong. I said, and they laughed. I cry myself to sleep at night. I have given hints to my brother, but can't tell anyone else in the family.

I am scared going to my Nan's and I think I have to go again this summer. He follows me everywhere and even if my Mum's around, he gives me looks. Help, please. Anon.

I understand how frightened and sad this makes you feel. You want to tell and you need to tell someone, but you need help in telling. If it's true you can't speak to Mum, then you need to try to talk to some other grown-up. Your friends at school and even your brother probably aren't going to be able to do enough. Who shall this grown-up be? Would you like to ring Childline – it's free – 0800 1111? Would you like to talk to a teacher? Someone who makes you feel confident, who smiles at you sometimes? Or could you tell the doctor? I don't think you should have to live the rest of your childhood in fear. If you ring Childline, you can discuss ways to make sure you aren't alone with your uncle ever again. And also ways to tell him to leave you alone anyway.

(Following the broadcast of this letter on *Going Live!*, 'Anon' rang Childline, told her Mum, and is now safe and well.)

Abused – dad

I watched the Growing Pains *part of the show this morning and thought you might be able to help me. My Dad has been abusing me since I was seven and a half and it's got worse as time has gone on. I try so hard not to make him angry when he's in my room, but he wants to be angry and it makes things better for him. I don't know what I do that makes him want to hurt me. I try to be good. I tried to talk to my Mum but she wouldn't let me say anything and she told me to be a good girl and not cause trouble. Now I'm older I'm frightened I will get pregnant so I told Dad to leave me alone. He went absolutely mad and hit me hard in the face and did other things. He hurt me so much I wanted to die. I had to stay home from school for over a week because I had a big bruise on my face where he hit me. He hardly ever hits me on the face, just where it won't show. My Mum's been staying with my Gran because she's been in hospital and things have become so awful – he comes in my room every night and sometimes in the morning. When I got him so mad, he told me I could easily disappear and he could say I'd run away and that thousands of kids disappear every year and their parents cannot find them. I'm so frightened and can't tell anyone because I'm scared he might kill me. I sometimes wish I wasn't here because I don't enjoy my life at all. Anon.*

What's being done to you makes me sick and I hope with all my heart you will be able to make a plan of escape. Your father is not only uncaring, he is extremely dangerous and sadistic.

I'm afraid your mother is not capable of looking after you either. Please believe me when I say you have done all that you could to cope with your parents and there is nothing bad about you at all, though I understand that you feel terrible inside.

You say to me that you are only prevented from ending the abuse because you are afraid of being killed. The only question, therefore, is not whether to go but how to get away. You will certainly need some help. First, you can ring Childline *free* on 0800 1111 to explore your options. Secondly, you can ring the NSPCC on their 24-hour-a-day service – 01-404 4447. They will talk to you in confidence – they won't try to trace your call. And when you feel ready to make the move, they will arrange to take you to a place of safety; your ordeal will be ended and you will never have to put up with your father's criminal behaviour again. The NSPCC have the money from the Government to look after you – please take action.

(The writer of this letter rang the NSPCC and is now safe.)

Wrong touch

Please help me. I have got this friend (male) who keeps touching me where he should not. I am sure he is gay and I try keeping away from him, but he follows me everywhere and he once asked me round to his house because his parents were out. I don't know what to do now. Anonymous Boy.

You *own* your body and only you can give permission for someone to touch it. So when this rule gets broken, you must speak up. 'Don't touch me like that, I don't like it' is the message. If the problem continues, tell someone who can intervene. You should never keep a secret that makes you feel screwed up.

Bullying thief

Recently, I've seen someone stealing. He knew I did, too. As I came out of the shop, he grabbed me and said if I told anyone, the worst would happen. I've been so afraid since then and I now make sure I go everywhere with my Mum. It's like a jail experience. Please help me overcome my problem and quickly. A Kylie fan.

Bad secrets always screw you up. Being bullied always screws you up. You need to tell someone what's on your mind. This is not the same as saying you have to be a policeman and get this other person caught. I think it's more important for you to feel your parents will protect you from the threats he's uttered. You can't go on living in terror – tell your Mum and Dad and leave it to them to look after you and this nasty little thief. PS – Esther Rantzen's new helpline 0800 010390 is also available for those being bullied.

Sexy phonecall

Please help, I'm dead worried. I rang one of those sexy stories for adults. I didn't think at the time, but the next day I saw this warning: 'These phone lines are of a sexually explicit nature – all calls at dialler's own risk.' Will the police get in contact with me? Help – NKOTB fan.

No, the police will not be involved unless your parents make a complaint. Even then, the phone service did issue a warning, so I doubt whether any action would result. But remember – these calls are expensive so your Mum and Dad might start asking you hard money questions.

Facing water

Every Thursday I go swimming with my class, but my worry is I cannot put my face in the water. Please could you give me some advice? Worried, 9.

Yes. Buy a nose clip, keep your eyes closed and take a big breath before you go under. Do it for a short time to get used to the feel and you'll be fine.

Hates PE

I am 11 years old and don't like games, PE, etc. It gets so bad that I even pretend to be ill when I'm not. Could you please help me because it's getting really bad and making me uptight. Jamie, Middlesborough.

I also tried skiving off games at school and you and I both know it doesn't work. So you're stuck with doing physical education.

It may help if you can decide why you hate games. Is it because you are too fat? (This was my problem.) Or is it because you don't know how to play them? Or is it because the teacher shouts at you?

Some of these problems you can control – going on a diet, learning the rules of football and practising your kick. Some you can't change (loud teachers, for instance).

But in any situation you can tell yourself the discomfort doesn't really last that long. If teachers pick on you, just count silently till they've done.

It's hell standing on the pitch with a freezing cold wind blowing up your shorts. But you will be home by tea.

Real dream?

Please help. I had a bad dream a few days ago. It was about a man who was trying to get me so I shot him in the head. I know you are probably thinking it was just a dream. Well, I thought so too, but I have seen this man recently in the street giving me a sly look as I pass by. I've told my Mum and a friend and they suggested writing to you. Please help me because I am not sleeping properly. Anon.

This dream is about your fear of attack. It probably began when you heard some story in the news about children being hurt. You may have seen this man in the street just for a second and *borrowed* his face for the dream. You may have been bothered by the violence of your dream. Now when you see the man in true life you feel both afraid *and* guilty. But dreams never mean to hurt us. They are trying to get us to face up to the world, which *is* a dangerous place. I think your dream is saying you don't want anyone to touch you and if they do, watch out!

CHAPTER 10

Extras

Wants a sign

*This is really not a serious problem but I'd love to know
the answer. My name is Gillian and I'm 11. My
birthday is on 21st June and I'm a Gemini. Or at least
I think I am since in some magazines and newspapers
I'm mostly Gemini but sometimes I'm down as Cancer.
Everyone says I should just read Gemini but if my
birthday is listed under the sign of Cancer, what should
I think? Gillian.*

My astrology friend (who has the wonderful name
of Shelley Von Strunckel) says the important fact is
the *time* of day you were born. From this an expert
could tell you whether you are really Gemini or
really Cancer. She says you can't be both.

The problem arises because astrology really follows the seasons rather than the calendar and the
calendar does not exactly fit (leap year and all
that).

Her suggestion is that you get hold of a magazine called *Prediction* and look at the ads from
companies offering to do your chart by computer,
then save up the £3 or £4 it will cost. They'll get it
right.

I'd only add: have you noticed how newspaper
horoscopes are never precise? Do you think that's
why they're never wrong?

Fame!

*Every time I watch telly and a girl or boy my age comes
on I get jealous because I would so much like to be on
telly. Please could you arrange something for me?
Jealous Debby.*

Personally no, because they haven't made me

Controller of BBC1 or BBC2 (silly them) and I don't actually produce a programme.

What you need to do is look in the *Radio Times* for the correct name of the producer of the programme you want to be on. Then write a very careful letter saying what a smash, fab, brill, mega-wonderful person they must be for making such a triffic show, and could you please be on stage in the audience next time they broadcast? *And don't give up if it doesn't work first time.*

RSPCA time

I fear I am allergic to Gordon the Gopher because every time he appears on the screen I sneeze. I enclose a gun (caps supplied). Please would you threaten Gordon for me to see if it would help? Ollie Karger.

No. Switch off your television instead.